SCHAUM'S *Easy* OUTLINES

ITALIAN

Other Books in Schaum's Easy Outlines Series Include:

SCHAUM'S *Easy* OUTLINES

ITALIAN

BASED ON SCHAUM'S
Outline of Italian Grammar
BY JOSEPH E. GERMANO, Ph.D.
AND
CONRAD J. SCHMITT

AND

Outline of Italian Vocabulary
BY LUIGI BONAFFINI,
FIORENZA CONSONNI CLARK,
AND
CONRAD J. SCHMITT

ABRIDGEMENT EDITOR
GLORIA ALLAIRE, Ph.D.

SCHAUM'S OUTLINE SERIES
McGRAW-HILL

New York   Chicago   San Francisco   Lisbon   London   Madrid
Mexico City   Milan   New Delhi   San Juan
Seoul   Singapore   Sydney   Toronto

The *McGraw·Hill* Companies

JOSEPH E. GERMANO is Associate Professor of Foreign Languages at the State University College in Buffalo, New York. A native of Italy, he received his Ph.D. in Italian from Rutgers University, New Brunswick, where he also coordinated the Rutgers Italian Workshop Series. He has written articles on Italian literature and culture, and was founder and co-editor of *NEMLA Italian Studies*.

CONRAD J. SCHMITT, the author of many foreign language books, was Editor-in-Chief of Foreign Languages, ESL, and Bilingual Publishing with McGraw-Hill Book Company. Before that, he taught languages at all levels of instruction from elementary through college, including Montclair State College, Upsala College, and Rutgers University, New Brunswick, and served as Coordinator of Foreign Languages for the Hackensack, New Jersey, Public Schools.

LUIGI BONAFFINI is a professor of Italian language and literature at Brooklyn College/CUNY. His publications include *La poesia visionaria di Dino Campana* and many translations of Italian poetry. He is also the author of a translation program for advanced Italian students.

FIORENZA CONSONNI CLARK, currently a teacher of Italian and Spanish at the Raritan High School in Hazlet, New Jersey, was born in Italy, received her teacher's certificate in Marche, Italy, and studied at the University of Rome. She also attended Rutgers University in New Brunswick, New Jersey.

GLORIA ALLAIRE directs the Italian program at the University of Kentucky. She received a bachelor's degree in music and M.A. and Ph.D. degrees in Italian from the University of Wisconsin, Madison. She is the author or editor of several books on Italian literature and has published numerous papers and encyclopedia articles on medieval, Renaissance, and women's studies topics.

1 2 3 4 5 6 7 8 9 0 DOC DOC 0 9 8 7 6 5 4

ISBN 007-142244-7

Contents

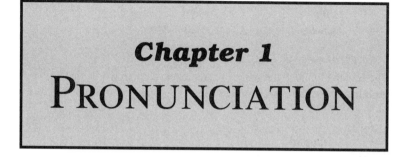

Chapter 1
PRONUNCIATION

The Italian Alphabet and Its Sounds

The Italian alphabet has only twenty-one letters: five vowels and sixteen consonants. Italian is a phonetic language: with few exceptions, words are pronounced as they are spelled. **H** is always silent. The vowels **e** and **o** can be either open or closed, and vary according to different Italian regional accents.

Dipthongs (two adjacent vowels) and tripthongs (three adjacent vowels) exist. In these combinations, a vowel may become a semivowel and lose its typical pronunciation. Each vowel maintains a value, however.

Dipthongs	*Tripthongs*
piuma	**miei**
uomo	**tuoi**

1

piano   **suọi**
Fięsole   **maiụscolo**

The Italian alphabet, the names for its letters, Italian words that use each letter, and the corresponding English pronunciation follow:

Letter	Italian Name	Italian Example	Approximate English Sound
a	*a*	**padre, mamma**	*father, ah!*
b	*bi*	**banạna, buọno**	*banana, bat* but with lips more compressed
c	*ci*	**cịnese, cinema**	*church, chop (See box.)*
d	*di*	**dove, divịno**	*dear, duet* but tongue is heavier against teeth
Open e	*e*	**bello, vento, è**	*letter, legible*
Closed e		**sete, bene, pepe**	*make, say*
f	*effe*	**fiụme, fuọri**	*foot, formal*
g	*gi*	**gita, Gino**	*Gene (See box.)*
h	*acca*	**ho, hai, hanno**	Initial **h** is always silent.
i	*i*	**così, divịno, Dio**	*cheese, please, green*
l	*elle*	**latte, lei, Luịsa**	*letter, love, Louise* but more tongue pressure against upper teeth.
m	*emme*	**mụsica, moto**	*music, mother*, but with lips more compressed
n	*enne*	**nonno, naso**	*none, nasal*
Open o	*o*	**cosa, donna costa, porta**	*lost, awful*
Closed o		**dopo, mondo dove, sole, ora**	*stony, lonesome*
p	*pi*	**papa, pio, padre**	*pope, pious, pin* but not aspirated
q	*cu*	**quattro, questo, quịndici, quọta**	*kw* sound as in *queen*
r	*erre*	**Roma, raro**	Single **r** is always flipped or trilled.
		arrivedẹrci, carro	Double **r** is rolled.

Letter	*Italian* *Name*	*Italian* *Example*	*Approximate* *English Sound*
s	*esse*	**suo, sito, subito**	Initial **s** always unvoiced: seldom, seen, someone.
		quasi, chiesa, paese **casa, rosa, frase**	Intervocalic **-s-** is mostly voiced (buzzed) in the North: zebra, but unvoiced in the South: Mississippi.
		risentire, girasole, **controsenso,** **sessantasei**	Unvoiced after prefixes or in compound words.
		ascoltare, discutere, **scala, scopa, scuola,** **spazio, stare, stoffa,**	Unvoiced (hissed) before any unvoiced consonant: spider, still.
		sbaglio, sdegno, **sdraia, sgabello,** **sgelo, slancio,** **slitta, smagrire,** **svanire**	Voiced before any voiced consonant: like **z** in zebra, zenith.
t	*ti*	**terra, tè, topo, pasta**	tire, take but less aspirated
u	*u*	**buco, luna, sugo**	cool, ruler
v	*vu (vi)*	**vino, vulcano, Vespa**	vote, vow
z	*zeta*	**Firenze, zio,** **pazienza**	
		pizza, stanza, **zucchero**	Mostly unvoiced, like the **ts** in vets.
		azzurro, mezzo, **ozono, romanzo,** **zero, zodiaco**	Some words voiced, as in beds.

Foreign Letters

Five additional letters are foreign to Italian, but do appear in words borrowed from other languages. There is an attempt to pronounce these as in the original languages; however, results do not always conform to the original.

Foreign Letter	Italian Name	Examples
j	*i lunga*	jolly, junior, jazz
k	*kappa*	hockey, kimono, poker
w	*doppia vu*	Walter, Wow!, whiskey
	(vu doppia)	wrangler
x	*ics*	box, taxi, unisex
y	*ipsilon; i greca*	derby, sexy, yoga

Note!

A few special spellings can be troublesome for speakers of English. However, these spellings will always be pronounced the same way, whether at the beginning of a word or internally.

The sound of English **ch** *(church)* appears in Italian as:
ci before **a, o** or **u**: **ciao, ciance, cioè, ciuffo**;
but **c** before **e** or **i**: **ceci, sincero, cinema, medici**.

The sound of English **k** *(key)* appears in Italian as:
c alone before **a, o,** or **u**: **caro, carne, come, cucina**;
but **ch** before **e** or **i**: **che, biblioteche, chi, Chianti**.

The sound of English **j** *(John, Joseph)* appears in Italian as:
g plus **i** before **a, o,** or **u**: **già, Giovanni, Giuseppe**;
but **g** alone before **e** or **i**: **gelo, gita**.

The sound of English **g** *(game, good)* appears in Italian as:
g alone before **a, o,** or **u**: **gatto, gonna, legume**;
but insert an **-h-** before **e** or **i**: **larghe, ghiaccio**.

The sound of English **sh** *(shoe)* appears in Italian as:
sci before **a, o** or **u**: **sciame, sciopero, sciupare**;
but **sc** before **e** or **i**: **esce, pesci, uscire**.

The sound of English **sk** *(sky)* appears in Italian:
sc before **a, o** or **u**: **scarpa, escono, scopo, scusi**;
but **sch** before **e** or **i**: **scherzo, pesche, Schicchi**.

Double Consonants

Any consonant may be doubled in Italian. In speaking, the sound of the doubled consonant is prolonged. Proper use of single or double pronunciation is vital to avoid giving an incorrect meaning. One learns to hear the difference. Note how meanings may change:

Single Consonant	*Double Consonant*
ala *wing*	**alla** *to the*
cane *dog*	**canne** *canes, reeds*
camino *fireplace*	**cammino** *roadway*
capello *a hair*	**cappello** *hat*
caro *dear*	**carro** *cart*
casa *house*	**cassa** *cash box*
lego *plastic toy*	**leggo** *I am reading*
nono *ninth*	**nonno** *grandfather*
pena *pain*	**penna** *writing pen*
sono *I am; they are*	**sonno** *sleep*
tufo *tufa, soil type*	**tuffo** *(n.) dive, plunge*

Syllabication

Unlike English syllables, which end in consonants, Italian syllables frequently end in a vowel sound. To properly divide Italian words in speech or when inserting hyphens in writing, follow these general guidelines:

1. A single consonant absorbs the vowel that follows:

   ca–de̦–re *to fall*
   ve–de̦–re *to see*
   pe̦–pe *pepper*
   ra–gio̦–ne *reason*

2. Most consonant pairs absorb the syllable that follows:

   pa̦–sta *pasta*
   ba̦–gno *bath, bathroom*
   fi̦–glia *daughter*
   va–ni̦–glia *vanilla*

BUT

L, **m**, **n**, and **r** are always divided from any other consonant that follows:

> **al–be–ro** *tree*
> **cor–sa** *race*
> **im–pe·ro** *empire*
> **man–cia** *tip (for a service person)*

3. All double consonants are divided:

> **bas–so** *short*
> **pan–na** *cream*
> **son–no** *sleep*
> **peg–gio** *worse*

4. When three consonants appear together internally (<u>not</u> initially), the first is absorbed by the preceding syllable:

> **sem–pli–ce** *simple*
> **den–tro** *inside*
> **Lon–dra** *London*
> **In–ghil–ter–ra** *England*

5. When the vowels **i** and **u** are unstressed, they will be absorbed by the vowel that follows:

> **chia–ve** *key*
> **chie–sa** *church*
> **chiu–so** *closed*
> **schiu–ma** *foam*
> **uo–mi–ni** *men*

Stress and Accent Marks

A large group of Italian words has accents on the penultimate (next to the last) syllable. This is one of the elements that gives Italian its musical "lilt."

> **bi–glie·t–to** *ticket*
> **ra–vio·li**
> **tre–no** *train*
>
> **cap–puc–ci·no**
> **spa–ghet–ti**
> **vi·–no** *wine*

However, many Italian words have their accent on an earlier syllable, the third or even fourth to the last. To properly determine where the accent falls on an unfamiliar word, it is always best to consult a dictionary.

cre–de–re *to believe* gon–do–la *gondola*
mu–si–ca *music* sim–pa–ti–co *nice, pleasant*
Ste–fa–no *Stephen* te–le–fo–na–no *they are telephoning*

In Italian, an accent is written mostly on final, accented vowels, rarely internally. Final vowels are accented for two reasons: because a syllable has disappeared in modern usage or the final syllable has been dropped from a foreign word.

Modern Usage	*Original Spelling*
città *city*	**cittade**
pietà *pity, compassion*	**pietade**
virtù *virtue*	**virtude**
comò *chest of drawers*	**commode**

You Need to Know ✔

Italian grammar books use the convention of a dot under the accented syllable to help students. Dots are not written in real Italian.

In writing, Italian used to make a distinction between acute (´) and grave (`) accents. Final accented **à** and **ò** always take the grave accent. These occur frequently in the singular forms of the future tense. Note that words with accented final vowels do not change in the plural.

à, ò always   **civiltà** *civilization(s)*
                  università *university, universities*
                  comò *chest(s) of drawers*
                  falò *bonfire(s)*

For accented **e**, the accent type once indicated whether the vowel was open or closed. Recently it has become acceptable to use the grave accent regardless of vowel or sound. Exceptions for which the acute accent are still preferred are **perché** (*why, because*) and **-tré** (*three*) at the end of a larger number. Here are some examples:

anziché *instead of*   **Cefalù** *Sicilian city*
cioè *that is to say*   **più** *more*
così *thus, so*   **dì** *day*

Remember

Always consult a good dictionary to be sure of spelling, meaning, where to divide a word into syllables, and which syllable receives the stress.

Chapter 2
NOUNS AND ARTICLES

IN THIS CHAPTER:

✔ *Gender*
✔ *The Indefinite Article*
✔ *The Definite Article*
✔ *Uses of the Definite Article*
✔ *Special Nouns*
✔ *Plural Spellings with **c** and **g***
✔ *Noun Suffixes*
✔ *Prepositional Contractions*
✔ *The Partitive*

Gender

Regular Nouns

Singular Forms

The Italian noun, unlike its English counterpart, has a gender. Nouns that refer specifically to males (*brother*, *uncle*, etc.) are masculine. Nouns that refer specifically to females (*sister*, *aunt*, etc.) are feminine. For other

9

nouns that have no actual gender (*book, fountain,* etc.), the categories "masculine" and "feminine" are still used, but arbitrarily.

Fortunately, the gender of many Italian nouns can be recognized by their endings. Almost all nouns that end in **-o** are masculine; almost all nouns that end in **-a** are feminine.

Masculine	*Feminine*
fratello *brother*	**sorella** *sister*
nonno *grandfather*	**nonna** *grandmother*
ragazzo *boy, guy*	**ragazza** *girl*
zio *uncle*	**zia** *aunt*
campo *field*	**casa** *house*
libro *book*	**fontana** *fountain*
museo *museum*	**amica** *female friend*

Hint ✔

To remember how endings reflect gender, think of Italian proper names you may know.
Masculine: **Gino, Francesco, Fabio.**
Feminine: **Gina, Francesca, Giovanna.**

Plural Forms

Italian does not form its plurals by adding an **-s** to nouns as some languages do. To form the plural of masculine nouns ending in **-o**, the **-o** changes to **-i**, and the feminine noun ending **-a** changes to **-e**.

fratello → fratelli	sorella → sorelle
libro → libri	casa → case

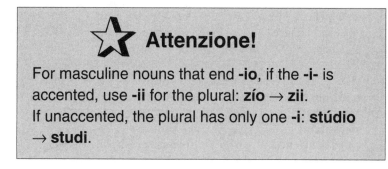

☆ Attenzione!

For masculine nouns that end **-io**, if the **-i-** is accented, use **-ii** for the plural: **zío** → **zii**. If unaccented, the plural has only one **-i**: **stúdio** → **studi**.

Nouns Ending in -e

A third category of noun (people, animals, or things) can be either masculine or feminine. The ending shows only if a noun is singular or plural. One must memorize the gender of nouns ending in **-e**.

Singular	*Plural*
cantante *singer*	**cantanti** *singers*
cane *dog*	**cani** *dogs*
giornale *newspaper*	**giornali** *newspapers*

Remember

Nouns ending in **-ione** are <u>always</u> feminine: **stazione** (*station*), **trasmissione** (*transmission*). Their plural is **-ioni**.

The Indefinite Article

Unlike English, in Italian the indefinite article (**a**, **an**) has four forms. These agree with the noun's gender and also facilitate pronunciation: **un** for most masculine nouns; **uno** for masculine nouns beginning with **z**, **ps**, or **s** plus a consonant; **una** for feminine nouns beginning with consonants; and **un'** for feminine nouns beginning with a vowel.

un fratello *a brother*   **una sorella** *a sister*
uno zio *an uncle*   **un'amica** *a female friend*
un giornale (*m.*) *a newspaper* **una stazione** (*f.*) *a station*

Many nouns that end in **-e** refer to people, either male or female. The article will show the actual sex of the person.

un cantante *a male singer*   **una cantante** *a female singer*
un paziente *a male patient*   **una paziente** *a female patient*
un parente *a male relative*   **una parente** *a female relative*

The Definite Article

There are several Italian equivalents for English *the*: **il, lo, la, l', i, gli, le**. In choosing which form to use, one must consider the gender and number of its noun as well as the beginning letters of the noun (to facilitate pronunciation).

Il is used before most masculine singular (m.s.) nouns.

> **il fratello** *the brother*
> **il libro** *the book*
> **il giornale** *the newspaper*

Lo is used before m.s. nouns beginning with **z**, **ps**, or **s** plus a consonant.

> **lo zio** *the uncle*
> **lo psicologo** *the psychologist*
> **lo studio** *the study*

La is used before feminine singular (f.s.) nouns beginning with any consonant or consonant cluster.

> **la sorella** *the sister*
> **la zia** *the aunt*
> **la studentessa** *the (female) student*

L' is used before m.s. or f.s. nouns beginning with a vowel.

> **l'esame** (*m.*) *the exam*
> **l'amico** *the male friend*
> **l'amica** *the female friend*
> **l'automobile** (*f.*) *the automobile, car*

There are two masculine plural articles. The plural form of **il** is **i** (used before most consonants). The plural of **lo** (before **z**, **ps**, **s** + cons.) or of **l'** (before vowels) is **gli**.

> **i fratelli** *the brothers*
> **i giornali** *the newspapers*
> **gli zii** *the uncles*
> **gli esami** *the exams*

The only feminine plural article is **le**. It is used before any consonant, consonant cluster, or vowel.

> **le case** *the houses*
> **le automobili** *the automobiles*
> **le trecce** *the braids*

 **Note!**

For nouns that end in **-e** (m. or f.), the gender must be memorized before the proper article can be assigned. Only the article clearly shows the gender of these nouns.

il cantante *the male singer*
la cantante *the female singer*
i cantanti *the male singers, or the male and female singers*
le cantanti *the female singers (women only)*

Uses of the Definite Article

With Titles

The definite article must be used with titles when talking about someone who is not present. In direct address, it is omitted.

Il dottor Cursietti è intelligente.

BUT

"Buon giorno, dottor Cursietti."

With General or Abstract Nouns

Unlike English, the Italian definite article is used with all general categories or abstract nouns. Compare:

I cani sono animali domestici. *Dogs are domestic animals.*
La pazienza è una virtù. *Patience is a virtue.*

With Languages

The definite article is used when referring to languages except after the verb **parlare** (*to speak*) and after the preposition **in**.

Parliamo inglese. *We speak English.*
Il documento è in spagnolo. *The document is in Spanish.*

With Family Members preceded by Possessive Adjectives

The definite article is commonly omitted with singular nouns denoting singular family members and relatives that are preceded by possessive adjectives (except **loro**). If the noun is modified with an adjective or suffix or if it is plural, the article must be used.

mia sorella (*my sister*)
la mia sorella minore (*my younger sister*)

la mia sorellina (*my dear little sister*)
le mie sorelle (*my sisters*)
la loro sorella (*their sister*)

With Days of the Week

Normally, days of the week are not accompanied by prepositions nor by articles: **Andiamo al cinema domenica**. (*We're going to the movies* [*this*] *Sunday*.)

To indicate a recurrent action ("on Sundays"), use the definite article: **Non c'è mai la scuola la domenica**. (*There's never school on Sundays*.)

With Place Names

The definite article is used with the names of continents, countries, large islands, chains of islands, regions, and rivers.

L'Africa è grande. *Africa is large*.
L'Italia è bella. *Italy is beautiful*.
Le Hawaii sono lontane. *The Hawaiian islands are far away*.
La Lombardia è nel nord. *Lombardy is in the north*.
Il Po è un fiume lungo. *The Po is a long river*.

The definite article is used with the prepositions **di** and **in** when the place name is modified or masculine.

Roma è nel Lazio.
Rome is in Lazio.
Venezia è una città del Veneto.
Venice is a city of the Veneto region.
Pisa è nella Toscana occidentale.
Pisa is in western Tuscany.

For unmodified feminine place names, the article is omitted.

Firenze è in Toscana. *Florence is in Tuscany*.
Pietro va in Sardegna. *Peter is going to Sardinia*.
I vini d'Italia sono ottimi. *Italy's wines are excellent*.

Special Nouns

Nouns Ending with an Accented Vowel

Masculine and feminine nouns ending with a stressed vowel do not change their ending in the plural. The article shows their number.

> **il caffè → i caffè**
> **la città → le città**
> **l'università → le università**

Abbreviations

Some nouns that appear to be irregular are actually just commonly used abbreviations. The article reflects the gender of the expanded form. In forming the plurals of abbreviations, only the article will change.

> **la bici(cletta)**   *"bike," bicycle* → **le bici**
> **la foto(grafia)**   *photo(graph)* → **le foto**
> **il cinema(tografo)**   *cinema(tograph)* → **i cinema**

Loan Words

Many words from other languages have entered into use in Italian. In general, these are simply considered masculine. The article is chosen based on the consonant or vowel that begins the word. Nothing is done to the end of the word to show number.

> **il computer → i computer**
> **il film → i film**
> **lo sport → gli sport**

Irregular Plural Nouns

Some nouns are completely irregular in the plural. These forms must be memorized.

l'**ala** (*wing*) → **le ali**
il **bue** (*ox*) → **i buoi**
il **dio** (*god*) → **gli dèi**
la **moglie** (*wife*) → **le mogli**
l'**uomo** (*man*) → **gli uomini**

Compound Nouns

Compound nouns are not as common in Italian as in some languages. When they occur, they may be formed by taking a verb root along with a noun to form a single word. When a verb is involved, the root is usually the third-person singular of the present indicative. Others unite two separate nouns or an adjective and a noun. The article always indicates the plural form; depending on the type, the noun's ending is not always inflected. Generally, only the second word changes to the plural, but exceptions do exist.

il **portacenere** (*ashtray*) → **i portacenere**
il **paracadute** (*parachute*) → **i paracadute**
il **capoluogo** (*capital city*) → **i capoluoghi**
l'**arcobaleno** (*rainbow*) → **gli arcobaleni**
la **ferrovia** (*railroad*) → **le ferrovie**
la **banconota** (*bank notes*) → **le banconote**
l'**altoparlante** (*loudspeaker*) → **gli altoparlanti**
la **cassaforte** (*safe*) → **le casseforti**

Masculine Nouns with Feminine Plurals

Many nouns, especially those which describe anatomy, follow a pattern that derives from the obsolete Latin neuter gender. In the singular, the noun and its article are clearly masculine, but in the plural the noun looks feminine singular and the article is feminine plural.

il **dito** (*finger, digit*) → **le dita**
il **braccio** (*arm*) → **le braccia**
il **lenzuolo** (*bedsheet*) → **le lenzuola**
il **paio** (*pair*) → **le paia**

Greek Borrowings

Singular Nouns Ending in -i

Some nouns seem to violate the above rules on gender and plural formation. This is because Italian developed mostly out of Latin, but a few
words have been borrowed from Greek and are therefore very irregular.

> **la crisi** → **le crisi** *crisis, crises*
> **la tesi** → **le tesi** *thesis, theses*

Masculine Nouns Ending in -a

For the same reason, one group of singular nouns ending in **-a** is really
masculine. Note spelling patterns in the singular: **-mma**, **-ma**, or **-ta**.
These words form their plurals regularly with **-i**.

> **il clima** (*climate*) → **i climi**
> **il programma** (*program*) → **i programmi**
> **il poeta** (*poet*) → **i poeti**
> **il pianeta** (*planet*) → **i pianeti**

Nouns for Professions

Certain masculine nouns that indicate professions become feminine by
changing their final vowel to **-a**. The article will also change.

> **il sarto** (*tailor*) **la sarta** (*dressmaker*)
> **il signore** (*gentleman*) **la signora** (*lady*)
> **il padrone** (*male owner*) **la padrona** (*female owner*)

Many masculine nouns ending in **-tore** have the corresponding feminine
ending **-trice**.

> **l'autore, l'autrice** (*author*)
> **lo stiratore, la stiratrice** (*presser*)
> **il lavoratore, la lavoratrice** (*worker*)

Some nouns indicating professions are formed on an originally French
suffix. The feminine form changes its article and final vowel.

il **cameriere** (*waiter*) la **cameriera** (*waitress*)
l'**infermiere** (*male nurse*) l'**infermiera** (*female nurse*)

Other names of professions incorporate the feminine pronoun **essa** to indicate the gender of the person.

lo **studente** (*student*) la **studentessa** (*female student*)
il **poeta** (*poet*) la **poetessa** (*female poet*)
il **conte** (*count*) la **contessa** (*countess*)

A large number of nouns that refer to professions end in **-ista**. In the singular, such nouns can refer to either a man or a woman, but the article clarifies the sex of the person. In the plural, both the article and the noun show the sex.

il **pianista** (*male pianist*)
la **pianista** (*female pianist*)
i **pianisti** (*male pianists, or mixed gender group*)
le **pianiste** (*female pianists only*)

Other nouns in **-ista** are: **artista, dentista, giornalista, farmacista, regista, telecronista, violinista**, etc.

Plural Spellings with c and g

Masculine

Masculine nouns that end in **-co** or **-go** may form their plurals in two ways: **-chi** or **-ci**; **-ghi** or **-gi**. In general, if the stressed syllable falls immediately before the final syllable, the plural ending will insert an **h** to maintain the hard consonant sound of the singular.

il **cuoco** (*cook*) → i **cuochi**
il **parco** (*park*) → i **parchi**
il **lago** (*lake*) → i **laghi**

In longer words where the accent falls on the antepenultimate (third to last) syllable, there is no **h** in the plural.

il mędico (*physician*) → i medici
l'aspạrago (*asparagus*) → gli asparagi

Nouns ending in **-logo** form their plural with **-ghi**.

il prọlogo (*prologue*) → i prologhi
il diạlogo (*dialogue*) → i dialoghi
il monọlogo (*monologue*) → i monologhi

There are always exceptions to these general guidelines.

l'amịco (*male friend*) → gli amici
il gręco (*Greek man*) → i greci
l'ọbbligo (*obligation*) → gli obblighi

Feminine

All feminine nouns that end **-ca** or **-ga** form their plurals with an **h**.

la biblioteca (*library*) → le biblioteche
la bottega (*boutique*) → le botteghe

Feminine nouns that end in **-cia** or **-gia** have two different plural spellings depending on whether the **-i-** is accented or not.

la dọccia (*shower*) → le docce
la guạncia (*cheek*) → le guance

BUT

la farmacịa (*pharmacy*) → le farmacie
la bugịa (*lie*) → le bugie

Remember

Always consult a good dictionary to be certain of irregular plural formation or unusual spellings.

Noun Suffixes

Diminutives: -uccio, -ello, -ino, -etto

When added to nouns or adjectives, these endings indicate smallness in size or convey a feeling of affection or endearment on the part of the speaker. Any suffix that ends -o has all four forms: -o, -a, -i, -e.

ragazzo *boy* → **ragazzino** *little boy*
vecchia *elderly woman* → **vecchietta** *dear old woman*
vino *wine* → **vinello** *a nice, light wine*
casa *house* → **casetta (casuccia)** *cute little house*

Augmentatives: -one

The masculine suffix **-one** indicates large size or importance. A feminine noun becomes masculine when this suffix is added. The plural of **-one** is **-oni**.

il libro *book* → **il librone** *large or important tome*
il ragazzo *boy* → **il ragazzone** *big, robust boy*
la minestra *soup* → **il minestrone** *hearty soup*

Pejoratives: -accio, -astro, -ucolo

A pejorative ending on a noun or adjective conveys a derogatory meaning. These suffixes have all four forms: -o, -a, -i, -e.

ragazzo *boy* → **ragazzaccio** *naughty boy*
parola *word* → **parolaccia** *vulgar word, curse word*

poeta *poet* → poetastro *hack poet*
maestro *teacher* → maestrucolo *poor instructor*

Caution!

In the early phases of learning the language, it is enough to simply recognize suffixes and the way they change a word's meaning. To avoid embarassment or unintended offense, it is advisable not to try adding these suffixes until one has a very strong command of the language.

Prepositional Contractions

Most Italian definite articles contract when used with common prepositions. The definite article always agrees with the gender and number of the noun it modifies. Prepositions never make agreements. Most prepositions simply combine with the definite article; however, small changes occur for reasons of pronunciation. Note that **di** becomes **de-** and **in** becomes **ne-**. The **l** of articles is doubled. All the modern contracted forms are shown below:

a + article = *to the, at the*
(*m. sing.*) **al, allo, all'**; (*f. sing.*) **alla, all'**; (*m. pl.*) **ai, agli**; (*f. pl.*) **alle**

da + article = *from the, by the,* or *to someone's place*
dal, dallo, dall'; dalla, dall'; dai, dagli; dalle

su + article = *on the*
sul, sullo, sull'; sulla, sull'; sui, sugli; sulle

di → de + article = *of the*
del, dello, dell'; della, dell'; dei, degli; delle

in → ne + article = *in the*
nel, nello, nell'; nella, nell'; nei, negli; nelle

Special Use of *da*

Da plus a person's name or title indicates to or at their residence or place of business.

Vado da Maria. *I'm going to Mary's (house).*
Ho un appuntamento dal dottore. *I have an appointment at the doctor's.*
Andiamo dai nonni. *We're going to (our) grandparents' (house).*

The Partitive

Indefinite quantity (*some, any*) is expressed by the preposition **di** plus the definite article. This is, in effect, the plural form of the indefinite *a* or *an*: **un libro** (*a book*) → **dei libri** (*some books*). The partitive is frequently used when referring to food items to indicate a portion. (See "Prepositional Contractions" above for all the possible forms.)

> **Prendo della minestra**. (*I'll have some soup.*)
> **Ecco dello zucchero**. (*Here's some sugar.*)
> **Mamma compra del pane**. (*Mother is buying some bread.*)

The partitive indicates an indeterminate amount of something. It is indefinite and imprecise.

> **Marco prende del caffè**. (*Mark is having some coffee.*)

The definite article conveys a general category or abstract meaning. Note that for such a meaning, English would omit the article. The definite article must be used whenever the noun is precisely described.

> **Gli piace il caffè**. (*He likes coffee* [in general].)
> **Gli piace il caffè Illy**. (*He likes Illy brand coffee.*)

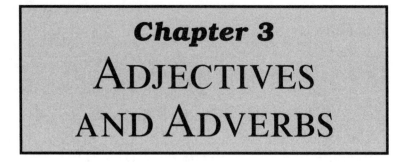

Chapter 3
ADJECTIVES
AND ADVERBS

✔ *Irregular Comparatives and Superlatives*
✔ *Absolute Superlative*

ADJECTIVES

Adjectives Ending in -o

Unlike English, most descriptive Italian adjectives follow the noun. Many commonly used Italian adjectives end in -o. These will always have four forms. Each of these adjectives must agree in gender and number with the noun it modifies.

Singular	*Plural*
l'appartamento moderno (*m.*)	**gli appartamenti moderni**
la casa moderna (*f.*)	**le case moderne**

Here is a list of some commonly used adjectives in -o.

allegro *cheerful, happy*	**generoso** *generous*
alto *tall*	**leggero** *light weight*
antico *old, ancient*	**maturo** *mature, ripe*
avaro *stingy*	**nuovo** *new* (for things)
basso *short, low height*	**pieno** *full*
bravo *good, proficient*	**povero** *poor* (all senses)
buono *good*	**ricco** *rich*
caldo *warm, hot*	**stretto** *narrow, tight*
freddo *cold*	**vecchio** *old*

As with nouns, masculine adjectives that end in **-co** or **-go** may form their plurals with or without an inserted **-h-**: **sporco, sporchi**, but **simpatico, simpatici**. Feminine adjectives that end in **-ca** or **-ga** <u>always</u> add an **-h-** in their plurals to preserve the hard sound of the singular: **stanca, stanche; lunga, lunghe**.

Another group of Italian adjectives ends in **-e**.

These show only number, i.e., singular or plural, and will have only two forms. These also typically follow the noun they modify.

Singular	Plural
il signore elegante (*m.*)	**i signori eleganti**
la signora elegante (*f.*)	**le signore eleganti**

Here is a list of some common adjectives that end in **-e**.

abile *able*	**forte** *strong*
breve *brief, short*	**grande** *large, great*
celebre *famous*	**importante** *important*
difficile *difficult*	**intelligente** *intelligent*
eccellente *excellent*	**interessante** *interesting*
facile *easy*	**triste** *sad*
felice *happy*	**veloce** *fast, speedy*

In Italian the adjective may be used without its noun, but with an article, to indicate a person of that given attribute.

un giovane *a youth*
gli anziani *the elderly*
i buoni e i cattivi *the good and the bad (people)*

Adjectives of Origin

Adjectives of origin referring to nationality, region, or state of origin always make agreements and follow the noun that they modify. As with the two adjective groups described above, these adjectives may have either four forms (**-o, -a, -i, -e**) or two (**-ese, -esi**) as shown:

Singular	Plural
il ragazzo americano	**i ragazzi americani**
la ragazza americana	**le ragazze americane**
l'uomo inglese	**gli uomini inglesi**
la macchina giapponese	**le macchine giapponesi**

Many adjectives of origin end in **-ese**. Here are more:

> **canadese** *Canadian*
> **cinese** *Chinese*
> **irlandese** *Irish*
> **olandese** *Dutch*
> **portoghese** *Portuguese*
> **svedese** *Swedish*

☆ ATTENZIONE!

Adjectives of origin are never capitalized in Italian.

When these adjectives are used to refer to the language spoken in that place, they are masculine singular.

Studio il francese.	*I'm studying French.*
L'articolo è in spagnolo.	*The article is in Spanish.*

Adjectives of Color

Adjectives used to describe color follow the same pattern. Those that end in -o have four forms and agree in both gender and number; those that end in -e have only two forms and only agree in number. Below are some examples:

azzurro, -a, -i, -e (*sky blue*)	**nero, -a, -i, -e** (*black*)
bianco, -a, -chi, -che (*white*)	**rosso, -a, -i, -e** (*red*)
giallo, -a, -i, -e (*yellow*)	**verde, -i** (*green*)

A few common adjectives of color are invariable (do not change endings). **Blu** is a French borrowing and does not change. Others are really nouns whose color is associated with the color being described.

> **arancione** *orange*, the fruit and its color
> **marrone** *chestnut*, the nut and its color
> **rosa** *rose*, the flower and its color
> **viola** *violet*, the flower and its color

Observe the lack of agreement with such adjectives:

> **la cravatta <u>blu</u>** *the blue tie*
> **la gonna <u>rosa</u>** *the pink skirt*
> **le gonne <u>rosa</u>** *the pink skirts*
> **il vestito <u>marrone</u>** *the brown suit*
> **i vestiti <u>marrone</u>** *the brown suits*

Adjective Forms Used before Nouns

We have seen that most adjectives follow the nouns that they describe. However, some commonly used adjectives can precede their nouns.

> **una donna bella = una bella donna** *a lovely lady*
> **un vino buono = un buon vino** *a good wine*

When this happens, certain adjectives have additional special endings used to facilitate pronunciation.

Bello

The positively charged adjective **bello** (*beautiful, handsome, wonderful, "great"* in the sense of quality) has more than four forms when it precedes a noun. Note how it resembles the forms of the definite article (**il, lo, la,** etc.). Once the adjective moves to its new position, the article may also have to be adjusted according to the proper rules of usage. (Refer to Chapter 2: The Definite Article.)

> *Singular*

> **il ragazzo, il <u>bel</u> ragazzo** *the handsome guy*
> **l'uomo, il <u>bell'</u>uomo** *the handsome man*
> **lo zaino, il <u>bello</u> zaino** *the really nice backpack*
> **la macchina, la <u>bella</u> macchina** *the beautiful (great) car*
> **l'estate, la <u>bell'</u>estate** *the wonderful summer*

Plural

i ragazzi, i <u>bei</u> ragazzi *the handsome guys*
gli uomini, i <u>begli</u> uomini *the handsome men*
gli zaini, i <u>begli</u> zaini *the nice backpacks*
le macchine, le <u>belle</u> macchine *the great cars*
le estati, le <u>belle</u> estati *the wonderful summers*

Bello is a very commonly used word in Italian daily life. These forms of **bello** before a noun are found in the exclamation of delight: **Che . . . !** Note that unlike English, the indefinite article is not used.

Che bella giornata! *What a lovely day!*
Che bel paesaggio! *What a beautiful landscape!*
Che belle bambine! *What beautiful little girls!*

Buono

The commonly used adjective **buono** refers to good moral character (people), good quality (objects), or good flavor (foods). When **buono** follows a noun, it has four forms: **buono, buona, buoni, buone**. It acquires two additional forms when it precedes certain <u>singular</u> nouns: **buon** before masculine nouns; **buon'** before m. or f. nouns beginning with vowels. This usage follows the rules for the indefinite article: **un, uno, una, un'**. (Refer to Chapter 2: The Indefinite Article.)

Singular

un ragazzo, un <u>buon</u> ragazzo *a good guy*
un uomo, un <u>buon</u> uomo *a good man*
uno zaino, un <u>buono</u> zaino *a good* (quality) *backpack*
una macchina, una <u>buona</u> macchina *a good car*
un'estate, una <u>buon'estate</u> *a good summer*

Plural

i ragazzi, i <u>buoni</u> ragazzi *the good guys*
gli uomini, i <u>buoni</u> uomini *the good men*
gli zaini, i <u>buoni</u> zaini *the good backpacks*
le macchine, le <u>buone</u> macchine *the good cars*
le estati, le <u>buone</u> estati *the good summers*

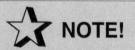

NOTE!

For an easy way to remember which common adjectives can precede the noun, think of the word **B-A-G-S: B̲eauty** (or Ugliness), **A̲ge**, **G̲oodness** (or Badness), and **S̲ize**.

Grande

In the singular, the adjective **grande** (great, large in size, or important) may be shortened to **gran** before masculine and feminine nouns that begin with a consonant other than **z**, **s** + consonant, or **ps**. With nouns beginning with **z**, **s** + consonant, **ps**, or a vowel, **grande** must be written out. The possibilities are shown below:

> **un gran signore** (*m.*) *a great gentleman*
> **una gran signora** (*f.*) *a great lady*
> **un grande artista** (*m.*) *a great (male) artist*
> **una grande artista** (*f.*) *a great (female) artist*
> **un grande zaino** (*m.*) *a large backpack*
> **un grande stadio** (*m.*) *a large stadium*
> **una grande stazione** (*f.*) *a large station*
> **un grande psicologo** (*m.*) *an important psychologist*
> **una grande psicologa** (*f.*)

Exception: note that **grande** becomes **grand'** before a masculine noun beginning with **u**: **un grand'uomo**. The plural form with all nouns, whether before or after, is **grandi**.

Santo

As with **grande**, **Santo** is shortened to **San** before masculine nouns, typically proper names, that begin with any consonant other than **z** or **s** + consonant. However, due to regional usage, at times **San** is used before such nouns. **Sant'** is used before all singular nouns that begin with a vowel. **Santa** is used for all singular feminine nouns that begin with a consonant. Some examples follow:

Santo Stefano
San Giuseppe
Sant'Anselmo (*m.*)
Sant'Anna (*f.*)
Santa Maria

The plural forms are regular: **santi** (*m.*) and **sante** (*f.*)

Demonstrative Adjectives

Demonstrative adjectives are used to point things out. In Italian as in English, demonstratives precede the noun. **Questo** (sing. *this;* plur. *these*) expresses closeness to the speaker, whether in actual spatial terms or affectively. **Questo** has four forms, plus elision with the apostrophe before singular *m.* or *f.* nouns that begin with a vowel.

questo cavallo	*this horse*	**questi cavalli**	*these horses*
questa chiesa	*his church*	**queste chiese**	*these churches*
quest'amico (*m.*)	*this friend*	**questi amici**	*these friends*
quest'amica (*f.*)	*this friend*	**queste amiche**	*these friends*

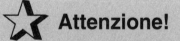 **Attenzione!**

Elision (dropping a final vowel and using an apostrophe) only occurs before a singular noun that begins with a vowel. Never elide plurals. This applies to articles, adjectives, pronouns, etc.

Quello (sing. *that;* plur. *those*) expresses spatial or affective distance from the speaker. **Quello** precedes all nouns. For this reason, adjustments to spelling must be made as for the adjective **bello** (see above). **Quello** has several forms similar to the definite article.

Singular		Plural	
il	quel ragazzo	i	quei ragazzi
lo	quello studente	gli	quegli studenti
	quello zio		quegli zii
	quello psicologo		quegli psicologi
l'	quell'amico (*m.*)	gli	quegli amici
la	quella ragazza	le	quelle ragazze
l'	quell'amica (*f.*)	le	quelle amiche

Possessive Adjectives

Possessive adjectives indicate ownership or possession. Their formation in Italian is more complex than in other languages. Each must agree with the noun it modifies in gender and number. In addition, Italian normally uses the definite article (not translatable) with the possessive adjective. All the possible forms appear below. **Tuo (-a, -i, -e)** means *your*, informal singular; that is, owned by one person. **Vostro (-a, -i, -e)** means *your*, informal plural; that is, owned by a group of people. **Suo (-a, -i, -e)** refers to *his*, *hers*, or *its*; it is "gender-free." **Suo** can also mean *your* in formal address and is often used in business correspondence to be respectful. Note that **loro** does not change its ending: it is really a subject pronoun.

	m. s.	*f. s.*	*m. pl.*	*f. pl.*
my	**il mio**	**la mia**	**i miei**	**le mie**
your	**il tuo**	**la tua**	**i tuoi**	**le tue**
his, her	**il suo**	**la sua**	**i suoi**	**le sue**
its				
ours	**il nostro**	**la nostra**	**i nostri**	**le nostre**
yours	**il vostro**	**la vostra**	**i vostri**	**le vostre**
theirs	**il loro**	**la loro**	**i loro**	**le loro**

il mio amico *my (male) friend*
la tua cravatta *your tie*
la sua casa *his, her, its, or your (formal) house*
il nostro cane *our dog*
la loro macchina *their or your (formal) car*
le mie scarpe *my shoes*
i suoi capelli *his, her, its, your (formal) hair*
i vostri vicini *your (informal) neighbors*

Caution!

The possessive adjective's ending agrees with the artificial gender and number of the **noun**, not with the true gender and number of the possessor (owner). A man or a woman would both say **il mio libro** (*my book*) or **la mia macchina** (*my car*): **libro** is a *m.s.* noun, but **macchina** is *f.s.*

Possessives with Family Members

When any grammatical form is used frequently, rules are broken and exceptions develop. We often refer to our close relatives, especially in the singular. In common usage, the definite article is dropped for these. Always maintain the article for all plural relatives and for **loro**. Always use the article if the noun is in any way modified.

Singular	*Plural*
mia sorella *my sister*	**le mie sorelle** *my sisters*
tuo marito *your husband*	**i tuoi cugini** *your cousins*
la loro sorella *their sister*	**le loro sorelle** *their sisters*
suo fratello *his/her brother*	
il suo fratello minore *his/her younger brother*	
la nostra zia generosa *our generous aunt*	

Comparatives of Equality

When comparing persons or things, the two may have equal characteristics: *John is <u>as</u> nice <u>as</u> Mary*. Italian has two equivalent expressions for this: **(così)** . . . **come** or **(tanto)** . . . **quanto**. The first word of each pair is often omitted, but the second is always used. The following sentences are identical in meaning:

> Giovanni è <u>così</u> simpatico <u>come</u> Maria.
> Giovanni è simpatico <u>come</u> Maria.

PISCES

> **Giovanni è <u>tanto</u> simpatico <u>quanto</u> Maria.**
> **Giovanni è simpatico <u>quanto</u> Maria.**
> *John is as nice as Mary.*

Note that when adjectives are used in a comparison, the adjective agrees with the first person or thing.

> **Maria è così simpatic<u>a</u> come Giovanni.**
> **I ragazzi sono simpatic<u>i</u> come le ragazze.**

Disjunctive pronouns are frequently used following a term of comparison.

> **Luisa è così alta come <u>lui</u>.**
> *Louise is as tall as he is.*
> **Roberto è tanto intelligente quanto <u>me</u>.**
> *Robert is as intelligent as I am.*

Nouns may also be used in comparisons of equality. In this case, only **tanto . . . quanto** may be used, and **tanto** must agree with the noun it precedes.

> **Giovanna ha tant<u>a</u> energia quanto sua sorella.**
> *Joann has as much energy as her sister.*
> **Questo museo ha tant<u>e</u> statue quanto l'altro.**
> *This museum has as many statues as the other.*

With verbs (actions), **così . . . come** and **tanto . . . quanto** are used alone after the verb without any other word intervening. In such statements, **così** and **tanto** are often dropped.

> **Tu ti vesti <u>così</u> <u>come</u> me.**⎫
> **Tu ti vesti <u>come</u> me.** ⎬ *You dress as I do.*
> **Antonio lavora <u>tanto</u> <u>quanto</u> lei.** ⎫ *Anthony works as*
> **Antonio lavora <u>quanto</u> lei.** ⎬ *much as she does.*

Comparatives of Inequality

Two persons or things being compared may be inequal in their attributes: *more than, less than.* Italian uses: **più . . . di, meno . . . di.** Such comparisons may involve adjectives, nouns, or verbs.

(*adj.*) **Giovanni è <u>più</u> simpatico <u>di</u> Maria.**
John is nicer than Mary.
(*n.*) **Questo museo ha <u>più</u> statue <u>di</u> quell'altro.**
This museum has more statues than the other one.
(*v.*) **Antonio lavora <u>meno di</u> lei.**
Anthony works less than she does.

Più di and **meno di** are used when the comparison is followed by a number.

Abbiamo <u>più di</u> cento dollari.
We have more than one hundred dollars.
Quel libro costa <u>meno di</u> quaranta euro.
That book costs less than forty euros.

The above comparisons involved one attribute shared by two different people or things. When two different attributes of the same person or thing are compared, Italian uses **che** instead of **di**: **più . . . che, meno . . . che.**

Questa città è <u>più</u> sporca <u>che</u> bella.
This city is dirtier than it is nice.
A Roma ci sono <u>meno</u> chiese <u>che</u> fontane.
In Rome there are fewer churches than fountains.
È <u>più</u> facile giocare <u>che</u> studiare.
It is easier to play than to study.

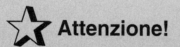 **Attenzione!**

When the comparison involves an action (shown by a verb) of a single person to his or her previous actions, the word order is reversed after the verb:

Ora Antonio lavora <u>di più</u>.
Now Anthony is working more.
Ieri Mauro ha scritto <u>di meno</u>.
Yesterday Mauro wrote less.

Relative Superlatives with Adjectives

The relative superlative of adjectives (*the most, the least*) is formed by using the appropriate definite article and the word **più** or **meno** before the adjective. Unlike the English relative superlative, which normally uses the preposition **in**, Italian always uses **di** ("of the," "belonging to the.") **Di** combines with the definite article, if needed.

> **Teresa è la più brava della classe.**
> *Theresa is the smartest in the class. (i.e., the class's smartest)*
> **Gino è il ragazzo meno atletico del gruppo.**
> *Gene is the least athletic boy in the group.*

As we have seen, many common adjectives (B-A-G-S) may come before or after the noun they modify. When these occur in a relative superlative, either position may be used, but the **più** or **meno** must also directly precede the adjective remaining together as a unit.

> **L'Alaska è lo stato più grande degli Stati Uniti.**
> **L'Alaska è il più grande stato degli Stati Uniti.**
> *Alaska is the largest state in the United States.*

Irregular Comparatives and Superlatives

The common adjectives **buono, cattivo, grande,** and **piccolo** have developed irregular forms for the comparatives and superlatives. These forms are completely interchangeable with the normal formation using **più (meno)** or the definite article plus **più (meno)**.

> **Questo vino è più buono.** = Questo vino è migliore.
> *This wine is better.*

> **Quei giocatori sono i più cattivi.** = Quei giocatori sono i peggiori.
> *Those players are the worst.*

Positive	Comparative	Relative Superlative
buono *good*	**migliore, -i** *better*	**il migliore** *the best*
cattivo *bad*	**peggiore, -i** *worse*	**il peggiore** *the worst*
grande *big*	**maggiore, -i** *bigger*	**il maggiore** *the biggest*
piccolo *small*	**minore, -i** *smaller*	**il minore** *the smallest*

Maggiore and minore may refer to actual physical size, to importance, or to age.

Giovanni è maggiore di sua sorella.
John is bigger (or older) than his sister.
Italo Calvino è tra i maggiori autori del Novecento.
Italo Calvino is among the greatest authors of the twentieth century.

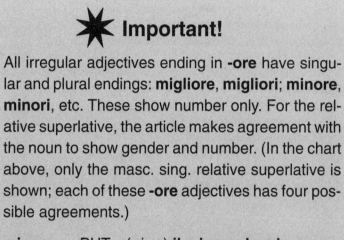

★ Important!

All irregular adjectives ending in **-ore** have singular and plural endings: **migliore, migliori; minore, minori**, etc. These show number only. For the relative superlative, the article makes agreement with the noun to show gender and number. (In the chart above, only the masc. sing. relative superlative is shown; each of these **-ore** adjectives has four possible agreements.)

minore   BUT   (*sing.*) **il minore, la minore**
minori   (*plur.*) **i minori, le minori**

Absolute Superlative

To give special emphasis to a person's or thing's attributes, the absolute superlative of an adjective is used. It adds the meaning *most, very,* or *extremely* to the quality being discussed. This is not a comparative expression; only one person or thing is mentioned. There are three ways to indicate this in Italian: by adding **molto** or **assai** before the adjective (note: **molto** and **assai** do not agree; **molto** always precedes the noun, **assai** may follow it); by doubling the short, common adjectives; and, for any adjective, by adding the suffix **-issimo (-a, -i, -e)** after dropping the final vowel. Study these examples:

> **La signora Agnelli è molto ricca.**
> **La signora Agnelli è assai ricca.** (= è ricca assai)

La signora Agnelli è <u>ricca ricca</u>.
La signora Agnelli è ricch<u>issima</u>.
Mrs. Agnelli is very rich.

When **-issimo** is added to an adjective that ends in **-e**, it will now have four possible endings instead of just two.

elegante (*sing.*)	**elegantissimo** (*m. sing.*)
	elegantissima (*f. sing.*)
eleganti (*plur.*)	**elegantissimi** (*m. pl.*)
	elegantissime (*f. pl.*)

For adjectives ending in **-co**, **-go**, **-ca**, and **-ga**, an **h** is always added before the **-issimo** to preserve the hard sound.

un uomo stanco *a tired man*
un uomo stan<u>ch</u>issimo *a very tired man*

un fiume largo *a wide river*
un fiume lar<u>gh</u>issimo *a very wide river*

ADVERBS

Formation of Adverbs in **-mente**

Adverbs modify verbs to indicate how, when, or where an action is performed. In Italian, adverbs generally follow the verb directly. Adverbs may have more than one word and are always invariable: they do not make agreements. Here are some common adverbs:

di solito *usually*	**spesso** *often*
presto *early*	**subito** *right away, at once*
sempre *always*	**tardi** *late*
a volte, qualche volta *sometimes*	

Many Italian adverbs are formed from adjectives by adding the suffix **-mente** to the singular form and making other spelling adjustments. This corresponds to the English adverbs formed with **-ly**: *happy* → *happily*. There are three categories: adjectives that end in **-o** change to the feminine form before adding **-mente**; adjectives that end in **-e** simply add the suffix; adverbs that end in **-le** or **-re** drop the final **-e** before adding the **-mente**.

Singular Adjective	*Adjusted*	*Adverb with -mente*
chiaro *clear*	**chiara**	**chiaramente** *clearly*
rapido *rapid, fast*	**rapida**	**rapidamente** *rapidly*
veloce *speedy*	**veloce**	**velocemente** *speedily*
triste *sad*	**triste**	**tristemente** *sadly*
regolare *regular*	**regolar-**	**regolarmente** *regularly*
naturale *natural*	**natural-**	**naturalmente** *naturally*

Irregular Comparatives and Superlatives

The commonly used adverbs **bene**, **male**, **molto**, and **poco** have irregular forms in the comparative and relative superlative. Meanings are identical and the words are interchangeable.

Adverb	*Comparative*	*Relative Superlative*
bene *well*	**meglio** *better*	**il meglio** *the best*
male *badly*	**peggio** *worse*	**il peggio** *the worst*
molto *a lot*	**più (di più)** *more*	**il più** *the most*
poco *a little*	**meno (di meno)** *less*	**il meno** *the least*

> **Marco ha fatto bene.** *Mark did well.*
> **Marcello ha fatto meglio.** *Marcello did better.*
> **Massimo ha fatto il meglio.** *Massimo did the best.*

You Need to Know ✔

Stylistically, when **più** or **meno** are used in a comparison, they are followed by the preposition **di**. When they end the clause or sentence, they are preceded by **di**.

Ugo ha mangiato <u>più di</u> Giovanni. *Hugh ate more than John.*
Ugo ha mangiato <u>di più</u>. *Hugh ate more (than usual).*
Ugo ha mangiato <u>di più</u>, ma ha bevuto <u>di meno</u>.
Hugh ate more, but drank less.

Absolute Superlative

As with adjectives, the adverbs **bene, male, poco**, and **molto** form the absolute superlative by dropping their final vowel and adding the suffix **-issimo** to indicate "very." However, adverbs never make agreements so these have only one ending: **-o**. The suffix **-issimo** is never added to an adverb ending in **-mente** nor to most other adverbs!

(bene) **Giochiamo benissimo**. *We play very well.*
(male) **Carlo canta malissimo**. *Carl sings very badly.*
(poco) **Sandra mangia pochissimo**. *Sandra eats very little.*
(molto) **Studiamo moltissimo**. *We study very much.*

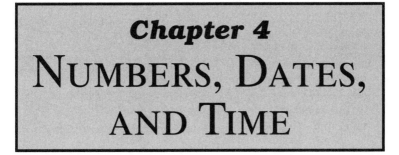

Chapter 4
NUMBERS, DATES, AND TIME

Numbers

Cardinal Numbers

The Italian cardinal numbers (used for counting, giving quantities) are shown below. The numbers from 11–19 are formed logically (1–9 plus 10), with some spellings adjusted for reasons of pronunciation. Underlined letters below indicate spellings to watch out for. Note that for 11–16, the notion of "10" is indicated by the suffix **-dici**; for 17–19, however, the number BEGINS with the prefix **dicia-**.

1 **uno**	11 **undici** (formed from **uno** + **dieci**)
2 **due**	12 **dodici** (**due** + **dieci**, etc.)
3 **tre**	13 **tredici**
4 **quattro**	14 **quattordici**
5 **cinque**	15 **quindici**
6 **sei**	16 **sedici**
7 **sette**	17 **diciassette**
8 **otto**	18 **diciotto**
9 **nove**	19 **diciannove**
10 **dieci**	

41

Numbers are invariable, that is, they do not change their endings to make agreements. The exception is **uno**, which agrees with the noun it precedes. This can mean either "a" or "one."

un libro e due penne	*a (one) book and two pens*
una penna e due libri	*a (one) pen and two books*
un'acqua minerale	*a (one) mineral water*
uno zaino e tre libri	*a (one) backpack and three books*

Here are the Italian numbers used in counting by tens. Note the suffix **-anta** for all numbers from 40–90.

20	**venti**	60	**sessanta**
30	**trenta**	70	**settanta**
40	**quaranta**	80	**ottanta**
50	**cinquanta**	90	**novanta**

After **venti**, **trenta**, **quaranta**, etc., the numbers **uno** through **nove** are simply attached at the end. Note that when using **uno** and **otto**, the final vowel elides. Numbers ending in **-tré** have a final acute accent.

21	**ventuno** (elision)	31	**trentuno**
22	**ventidue**	32	**trentadue**
23	**ventitré**	33	**trentatré**
24	**ventiquattro**	34	**trentaquattro**
25	**venticinque**	35	**trentacinque**
26	**ventisei**	36	**trentasei**
27	**ventisette**	37	**trentasette**
28	**ventotto** (elision)	38	**trentotto**
29	**ventinove**	39	**trentanove**

REMEMBER

When learning a language, always look for patterns.

In Italian the word **cento** (*hundred*) is invariable. Unlike English, the word *one* is not used in Italian: 100 = **cento**. Large numbers (hundreds, thousands, millions) are usually written out as one long word in Italian. To show 200, 300, 400, etc., simply add **due**, **tre**, **quattro**, etc. to the word **cento**. Spellings are very regular here.

100 **cento**	600 **seicento**
200 **duecento**	700 **settecento**
300 **trecento**	800 **ottocento**
400 **quattrocento**	900 **novecento**
500 **cinquecento**	

For the intervening numbers, just add whatever compounded number form is normally used to the word indicating hundreds.

110 **centodieci**
223 **duecentoventitré**
345 **trecentoquarantacinque**
456 **quattrocentocinquantasei**
567 **cinquecentosessantasette**
678 **seicentosettant̲o̲tto** ⎫
789 **settecent̲o̲ttantanove** ⎭   (Note the elisions)

In Italian the word **mille** (*one thousand*) also drops the word for *one*. Note that, unlike for hundreds, for multiple thousands there is a special plural form, **-mila**. The number is always said as it is written: 1,100 is pronounced **millecento**. (There is no way to say "eleven hundred" as in English.) Note that for large numbers, Italian uses a period where English would use a comma. For fractions, a comma is used where English would use a decimal point: Italian **8,5** (English *8.5*).

1.000 **mille**
2.000 **duemila**
3.000 **tremila**
5.100 **cinquemilacento**
6.250 **seimiladuecentocinquanta**
7.375 **settemilatrecentosettantacinque**

The numbers for *million* and *billion* have singular and plural forms. Note that here, like English, Italian does use the word *one*. These large numbers are not connected when written in words.

1.000.000 **un milione**	1.000.000.000 **un miliardo**
2.000.000 **due milioni**	2.000.000.000 **due miliardi**

Unlike smaller numbers, the numbers *one million* and higher insert the preposition **di** before a noun.

100 biglietti *one hundred tickets*
2.500 spettatori *two thousand five hundred spectators*
3.000.000 di dollari *three million dollars*
5.000.000.000 di euro *five billion euros*

Ordinal Numbers

Ordinal numbers (*first, second, third*, etc.) are used to indicate position within a category. The Italian ordinal numbers function as adjectives and must agree in gender and number with the nouns they modify: **la prima donna, l'atto secondo, i primi studenti**. The first ten ordinal numbers must be memorized.

1st **primo, prima, primi, prime**
2nd **secondo, seconda, secondi, seconde**
3rd **terzo, terza, terzi, terze**
4th **quarto (-a, -i, -e)**
5th **quinto (-a, -i, -e)**
6th **sesto (-a, -i, -e)**
7th **settimo (-a, -i, -e)**
8th **ottavo (-a, -i, -e)**
9th **nono (-a, -i, -e)**
10th **decimo (-a, -i, -e)**

The ordinal numbers *11th* and above add the suffix **-esimo (-a, -i, -e)** to the cardinal numbers. Numbers ending in **-tré** drop the accent, but keep the final **-e**. Numbers ending in **-sei** drop the final **-i**, but keep the **-e**. For ordinal forms in *thousands*, **-mille** is always used, not **-mila**.

11th **undicesimo (-a, -i, e)**
12th **dodicesimo (-a, -i, e)**
13th **tredicesimo (-a, -i, e)**
14th **quattordicesimo (-a, -i, e)**
33rd **trentatreesimo (-a, -i, e)**
56th **cinquantaseesimo (-a, -i, e)**
200th **duecentesimo (-a, -i, e)**
3000th **tremillesimo (-a, -i, e)**

Ordinal numbers of any size may be written with a cardinal number and superscripted letter to indicate agreement.

la terza (3^a) pagina *the third page*
il centesimo (100°) miglio *the hundredth mile*
il millesimo (1.000^o) posto *the thousandth seat*

Ordinal Numbers with Titles

To indicate numerical succession of kings, popes, emperors, etc., the ordinal numbers are written as capitalized Roman digits without a superscripted letter. These are read using the proper ordinal form with agreement.

as written	*as read*
Umberto I	*Umberto Primo*
Carlo V	*Carlo Quinto*
Leone X	*Leone Decimo*
Luigi XIV	*Luigi Quattordicesimo*
Elisabetta II	*Elisabetta Seconda* (note the feminine form)

Indicating Centuries

In historical accounts, there are several ways to indicate centuries in Italian. As in English, the ordinal number may be used. Italian also has a very common method of using the cardinal numbers that does not correspond to English usage: **il secolo tredicesimo, il tredicesimo secolo, il sec. XIII, il XIII sec.**, or **il Duecento** all refer to the thirteenth century. **Il Duecento** is an abbreviation of **milleduecento**. When this is done to show a century, the number is capitalized.

the fourteenth century ("the 1300s"):
il secolo quattordicesimo   **il sec. XIV**   **il Trecento**
il quattordicesimo secolo   **il XIV sec.**

the fifteenth century ("the 1400s"):
il secolo quindicesimo   **il sec. XV**   **il Quattrocento**
il quindicesimo secolo   **il XV sec.**

the twentieth century:
il secolo ventesimo   **il sec. XX**   **il Novecento**
il ventesimo secolo   **il XX sec.**

Fractions
Fractions are a mixture of cardinal and ordinal numbers.

1/4	**un quarto**	*one-fourth*
2/3	**due terzi**	*two-thirds*
3/8	**tre ottavi**	*three-eighths*

There are two ways to indicate *one-half*: the adjective **mezzo, -a** or the noun **una metà, la metà**.

> **Prendo un mezzo litro.** I'll take a half-liter.
> **Beviamo una mezza bottiglia.** We're drinking a half bottle.
> **Ne ho comprato la metà.** I bought half (of it).

Dates

The days of the week, the months, and the seasons of the year are not capitalized in Italian.

Days of the Week

All the days of the week are masculine, except **domenica**. Note that on the Italian calendar, Monday begins the week. The name of the day alone includes the notion of "this ..." or "on ....": **lunedì** can mean "this Monday" or "on Monday." Notice, however, that Italian never uses the preposition "on" with a day of the week.

lunedì *Monday*	**venerdì** *Friday*
martedì *Tuesday*	**sabato** *Saturday*
mercoledì *Wednesday*	**domenica** *(f.) Sunday*
giovedì *Thursday*	

Sabato pulisco la casa.
(This) Saturday I'm cleaning the house.
Domenica andiamo allo zoo.
(This) Sunday we're going to the zoo.

For actions that regularly recur on one day, the definite article is added.

Il sabato pulisco la casa.
On Saturdays I clean the house.
La domenica andiamo allo zoo.
On Sundays (regularly) we go to the zoo.

Months of the Year

All the months are masculine. Normally no article is used.

gennaio *January*	**luglio** *July*
febbraio *February*	**agosto** *August*
marzo *March*	**settembre** *September*
aprile *April*	**ottobre** *October*
maggio *May*	**novembre** *November*
giugno *June*	**dicembre** *December*

Dates throughout Europe are written: *day/month/year*, Italians sometimes use a Roman numeral for the month. Periods may be used to indicate divisions: **24/5/89**, **24.V.89** (May 24, 1989). When reading or saying a date, the definite, masculine singular article is used; when writing a date, the article is not written. When saying dates, cardinal numbers are used, except for the first of the month which is an ordinal number. The preposition **di** may be added between the day and the month. Common expressions that refer to the day or date follow.

Che giorno è oggi? *What day is today?*
–Oggi è martedì. *Today is Tuesday.*

Quanti ne abbiamo oggi? ⎫
Qual è la data di oggi? ⎬ *What's today's date?*
−Oggi è il 4 luglio. *Today is the Fourth of July.*
il quattordici (di) giugno *the fourteenth of June*
il trenta settembre *the thirtieth of September*
il primo (di) dicembre *December first*

Seasons of the Year

la primavera (*f.*) *spring*
l'estate (*f.*) *summer*
l'autunno (*m.*) *autumn, fall*
l'inverno (*m.*) *winter*

All the seasons can take the preposition **in**. The elided preposition **di** can be used with *estate* and *inverno*.

in primavera *in the spring(time)*
in estate (= **d'estate**) *in the summer(time)*
in autunno *in the fall*
in inverno (= **d'inverno**) *in winter*

When referring to a specific season of a particular year, the definite article is used: **Siamo andati in Italia nella primavera del 1998**. (*We went to Italy in the spring of 1998.*)

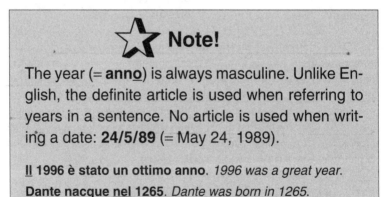

☆ Note!

The year (= **anno**) is always masculine. Unlike English, the definite article is used when referring to years in a sentence. No article is used when writing a date: **24/5/89** (= May 24, 1989).

Il 1996 è stato un ottimo anno. *1996 was a great year.*
Dante nacque nel 1265. *Dante was born in 1265.*

Time

Italians usually write the time (hour, minutes) with a period, not a colon. Hours (**ora, -e**) are feminine in Italian. The noun for "hour" is dropped, but the articles indicate the gender. *One o'clock* is singular; all the other times are plural because there are more than one hour.

> **È l'una**. *It's one (o'clock).*
> **Sono le due**. *It's two. (Literally, "They are two.")*
> **Sono le tre**. *It's three.*
> **Sono le quattro**. *It's four.*

Noon (**mezzogiorno**) and midnight (**mezzanotte**) count as singular when the special nouns for those times are used:

> 12.00 **Sono le dodici**. *It's twelve (o'clock).*
> **È mezzogiorno**. *It's noon* (literally, *midday*).
> **È mezzanotte**. *It's midnight.*

Minutes are added to the hour (up to the half hour) following the conjunction **e** (*and*). Minutes before the hour are subtracted (**meno** = *minus*) up to the half hour. The phrase **un quarto** (*a quarter*) commonly replaces "15 minutes." The phrase **e mezzo** refers to the half hour.

Times after the hour
> 1.05 **È l'una e cinque**. It's 1:05.
> 2.15 **Sono le due e quindici.** ⎱ It's 2:15.
>   **Sono le due e un quarto.** ⎰
> 3.25 **Sono le tre e venticinque**. It's 3:25.

One may use **e** plus the minutes (adding) up to 59, but this is not as commonly done: 3.45 = **Sono le tre e quarantacinque**.

Times before the hour
> 4.40 **Sono le cinque meno venti**.
> 6.45 **Sono le sette meno un quarto (meno quindici)**.
> 7.50 **Sono le otto meno dieci**.

Official Time

To avoid confusion, the 24-hour system ("military time") is used for nearly everything in Italy: transportation schedules, store hours, entertainment listings, etc. The use of A.M. or P.M. is unnecessary. Unlike American military time in which 14:00 is read "fourteen hundred hours," Italians simply use the cardinal numbers from 1 to 24. In this system, minutes are always added; they are never subtracted from the preceding hour. 9.00 = **Sono le nove**. *It's nine (in the morning)*, BUT 21.00 = **Sono le ventuno**. *It's nine (in the evening)*.

Colloquial Time

In daily conversation when times are given informally, Italians do use the twelve-hour clock. To be precise and avoid misunderstandings in this system, additional phrases are added.

di mattina	*in the morning*
del pomeriggio	*in the afternoon*
di sera	*in the evening*

Other Expressions

The question *What time is it?* has a singular or plural version: **Che ora è?** or **Che ore sono?** These may be used interchangeably.

Che ore sono?	*What time is it?*
–**È l'una.**	*It's 1:00.*
(or) **Sono le sette e mezzo**.	*It's 7:30.*

To ask *at what time* something occurs, one must add the preposition **a** to the definite article in both the question and the answer. English normally omits this preposition in the question.

A che ora pranziamo? (*At*) *what time are we having lunch?*
–**All'una e mezzo.** (*At*) *1:15.* (Note the elision with **una**.)

A che ora parte il treno? (*At*) *what time does the train leave?*
–**Parte alle 20.05 in punto**. *It leaves at 8:05 p.m., sharp.*

A che ora comincia il film? *At what time does the film begin?*
–**Comincia alle 21.15**. *It begins at 9:15 in the evening.*

Chapter 5
VERBS

IN THIS CHAPTER:

- ✔ Formal versus Familiar Forms
- ✔ Simple Tenses
- ✔ Imperfect Indicative
- ✔ Preterit Tense
- ✔ The Future Tense
- ✔ Compound Tenses
- ✔ The Subjunctive
- ✔ Reflexive and Reciprocal Verbs
- ✔ The Imperative (Familiar and Formal)
- ✔ The Gerund versus the Infinitive
- ✔ The Passive Voice

A verb is a word that indicates an action or a state of being. Italian verbs show more information in a single word than English. In English, a subject pronoun such as *I*, *you*, *he*, or *she* is used. In Italian, the subject pronouns are usually omitted since the ending of the verb changes in order to indicate the doer of the action. Furthermore, to form various tenses English must use auxiliary verbs such as *have, had, will,* or *would.* In Italian, instead of these extra words, a suffix or ending is added to the verb stem to indicate the tense.

    To form tenses in Italian, one must learn how the stem is formed and which set of endings to attach. In Italian, there are three main groups or categories of verbs. These are called "conjugations." Infinitives of first conjugation verbs end in **-are**; second conjugation verbs end in **-ere**; and third conjugation verbs end in **-ire**. A few minor groups also exist, and examples appear in this chapter. Even the so-called irregular verbs often have characteristics in common and can be grouped together to facilitate learning.

Formal versus Familiar Forms

Even though subject pronouns are generally not used, they can be added for extra emphasis and should be recognized. Italian makes a distinction in forms of address. When addressing friends, relatives, children or peers, informal (familiar) forms of the subject pronoun and verb are used. When addressing strangers, people you do not know well, shopkeepers, or older people, formal forms are used to show respect and to be polite. Notice that there are pronouns for formally addressing just one person (singular) or two or more people (plural).

Singular Subject Pronouns	*Plural Subject Pronouns*
io *I*	**noi** *we*
tu *you* (informal)	**voi** *you* (informal)
lui *he*	**loro** *they*
lei *she*	
Lei *you* (formal)	**Loro** (formal)

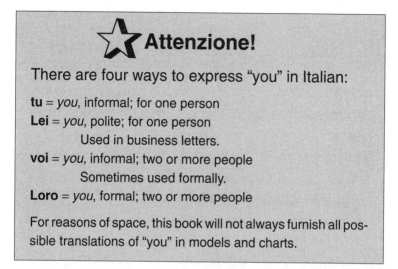

Attenzione!

There are four ways to express "you" in Italian:

tu = *you*, informal; for one person
Lei = *you*, polite; for one person
      Used in business letters.
voi = *you*, informal; two or more people
      Sometimes used formally.
Loro = *you*, formal; two or more people

For reasons of space, this book will not always furnish all possible translations of "you" in models and charts.

Notice that Italian has no regular pronoun for *it*. Other subject pronouns, now mostly obsolete, are still seen in formal writing: **egli** (*he*), **ella** or **essa** (*she*), **essi** (*m. pl., they*), and **esse** (*f. pl., they*). These may be used when it is necessary to refer to an inanimate object (*it, they*).

Simple Tenses

Present Indicative Tense (*Presente Indicativo*)

Regular First Conjugation Verbs (*-are*)
Many frequently used Italian verbs belong to this category. A partial list of such infinitives appears below.

abitare *to live, inhabit*	**guardare** *to look, watch*
alzare *to raise, lift up*	**guidare** *to drive*
amare *to love*	**imparare** *to learn*
arrivare *to arrive*	**informare** *to inform*
ballare *to dance*	**lavare** *to wash*
cantare *to sing*	**lavorare** *to work*
comprare *to buy*	**mandare** *to send*
cucinare *to cook*	**parlare** *to speak*
desiderare *to desire*	**salutare** *to greet*
firmare *to sign*	**suonare** *to play (music)*
giocare *to play (sports)*	**telefonare** *to telephone*

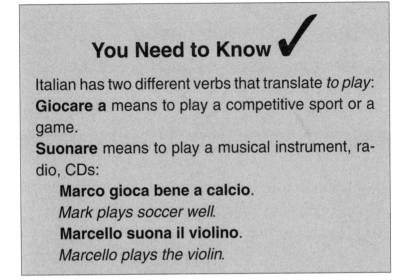

You Need to Know ✔

Italian has two different verbs that translate *to play*:
Giocare a means to play a competitive sport or a game.
Suonare means to play a musical instrument, radio, CDs:

Marco gioca bene a calcio.
Mark plays soccer well.
Marcello suona il violino.
Marcello plays the violin.

The present indicative tense of **-are** verbs refers to actions in the present or still to come (future). To form the stem, drop the **-are**; then add the verb endings to show the doer: **-o, -i, -a, -iamo, -ate, -ano.** (These endings are not the same as the ones for nouns and adjectives which show gender and number.) Observe:

Infinitive:	**comprare**	**parlare**
Stem:	**compr-**	**parl-**

compro *I buy*	**parlo** *I speak*
compri *you buy*	**parli** *you speak*
compra *he, she buys* *you* (formal) *buy*	**parla** *he, she speaks* *you* (formal) *speak*
compriamo *we buy*	**parliamo** *we speak*
comprate *you buy*	**parlate** *you speak*
comprano *they buy*	**parlano** *they speak*

There are three ways to translate the present indicative in Italian: **Compro** = *I buy* OR *I am buying* OR *I do buy*. It can also indicate a future action: *I will buy*.

Since verb endings are distinctive and change to show the person who is doing the action, subject pronouns are usually omitted. Subject pronouns are used for emphasis or clarity.

Lui chiama le ragazze. *He is calling the girls.*
Io arrivo alle otto, ma lei arriva alle dieci.
I am arriving at eight, but she will arrive at ten.

Verbs in *-ciare, -giare, -chiare, -ghiare*

Like all regular first conjugation verbs, these drop the **-are** before adding endings. The **-i-** in the **tu** and **noi** forms does not double. One must keep the **-h-** in the **-chiare** and **-ghiare** verbs. Study:

Infinitive: **cominciare**	**viaggiare**	**invecchiare**
Meaning: to begin	*to travel*	*to grow old*
Stem: **cominci-**	**viaggi-**	**invecchi-**
comincio	**viaggio**	**invecchio**
cominci	**viaggi**	**invecchi**
comincia	**viaggia**	**invecchia**
cominciamo	**viaggiamo**	**invecchiamo**
cominciate	**viaggiate**	**invecchiate**
cominciano	**viaggiano**	**invecchiano**

Verbs in *-care* and *-gare*

All verbs ending in **-care** and **-gare** add an **-h-** in the **tu** and **noi** forms to preserve the hard sound of the **c** or **g** as in the infinitive.

Infinitive:	**cercare**	**pagare**
Meaning:	*to search for*	*to pay for*
Stem:	**cerc-**	**pag-**
	cerco	**pago**
	cerchi	**paghi**
	cerca	**paga**
	cerchiamo	**paghiamo**
	cercate	**pagate**
	cercano	**pagano**

Other verbs of this type include: **allargare** *to widen*; **allungare** *to lengthen*; **attaccare** *to attack*; **frugare** *to rummage*; **indagare** *to investigate*; **sbarcare** *to disembark*; **toccare** *to touch*.

Regular Second Conjugation Verbs (*-ere*)

The infinitives of second conjugation verbs end in **-ere**. The present indicative tense of these verbs is formed by dropping the **-ere** and then adding the personal endings: **-o**, **-i**, **-e**, **-iamo**, **-ete**, **-ono**. Note that while the formation is similar to first conjugation verbs, the endings vary slightly for the **lui/lei**, **voi**, and **loro** forms. Asterisks indicate the differing forms.

Infinitive:	**correre**	**prendere**
Meaning:	*to run*	*to take*
Stem:	**corr-**	**prend-**
	corro	**prendo**
	corri	**prendi**
	corre*	**prende***
	corriamo	**prendiamo**
	correte*	**prendete***
	corrono*	**prendono***

Below is a list of commonly used **-ere** verbs followed by some examples of their use in sentences.

battere *to beat, hit*		**mettere** *to put, place*	
cadere *to fall*		**offendere** *to offend*	
chiedere *to ask*		**perdere** *to lose*	
conoscere *to be acquainted with*		**piangere** *to cry*	
credere *to believe*		**promettere** *to promise*	
involgere *to wrap*		**ricevere** *to receive*	
leggere *to read*		**scrivere** *to write*	

Conosci quell'uomo? *Do you know that man?*
Leggiamo il giornale. *We're reading the newspaper.*
Quel bambino piange sempre. *That child is always crying.*
Scrivo una lettera. *I am writing a letter.*

Verbs ending in *-cere*

Note the spelling changes for verbs that end in **-cere** are conjugated in the present indicative tense. This is to maintain the soft **c** sound of the infinitive. Other such verbs are: **compiacere** *to gratify, to please*; **dispiacere** *to displease*; and **giacere** *to lie down*.

Infinitive:	**piacere**	**tacere**
Meaning:	*to please*	*to be quiet*
Stem:	**piac-**	**tac-**

piaccio	**taccio**
piaci	**taci**
piace	**tace**
piac(c)iamo	**tac(c)iamo**
piacete	**tacete**
piacciono	**tacciono**

Regular Third Conjugation Verbs (*-ire*)

The infinitives of regular third conjugation verbs end in **-ire**. The present indicative stem is formed by dropping the **-ire** and adding the third conjugation endings: **-o, -i, -e, -iamo, -ite, -ono**. Note that these are similar to **-ere** endings except for the **voi** form. Asterisks indicate forms that differ from **-are** and **-ere** verbs.

Infinitive:	**aprire**	**partire**
Meaning:	*to open*	*to leave*
Stem:	**apr-**	**part-**

apro	**parto**
apri	**parti**
apre	**parte**
apriamo	**partiamo**
aprite*	**partite***
aprono	**partono**

Some commonly used regular **-ire** verbs are:

bollire *to boil*	**scoprire** *to discover*
coprire *to cover*	**seguire** *to follow*
dormire *to sleep*	**sentire** *to hear, feel, smell*
offrire *to offer*	**vestire** *to dress*

Third Conjugation Verbs with *-isc-*

When forming the present indicative, many **-ire** verbs add the infix **-isc-** after the normal stem and before the ending. They do this for all forms except **noi** and **voi**. Study the following as a model:

Infinitive:	**capire**
Meaning:	*to understand*
Stem:	**cap-**

io	**cap + isc + o = capisco**
tu	**capisci**
lui/lei	**capisce**
noi	**capiamo** (no **-isc-**)
voi	**capite** (no **-isc-**)
loro	**capiscono**

The following is a partial list of **-isc-** verbs:

apparire *to appear, to seem*
costruire *to construct*
differire *to differ, be different*
dimagrire *to lose weight*
finire *to finish*
ingrandire *to enlarge*
preferire *to prefer*
pulire *to clean*

Irregular Verbs in the Present
Many common verbs have become irregular through frequent use. This can be frustrating to a language learner, but these verbs must be memorized because the forms break the rules or follow different patterns than the regular verbs do. Verbs may be entirely regular in one tense, but irregular in others. Sometimes they maintain certain forms that are regular, but others are not, even within a single tense.

Avere *to have*
Note that **avere** is only regular in the **voi** form. The initial **h-** is silent on four of its present tense forms.

ho *I have*	**abbiamo** *we have*
hai *you have*	**avete** *you (all) have*
ha *he/she/it has*	**hanno** *they have*

Essere *to be*

The very common verb **essere** is entirely irregular. Note that **io** and **loro** use the same form: **sono**. This is usually clear in context, but the subject pronoun may be used for clarity. The accent on the **lui/lei** form must be written.

sono *I am*	**siamo** *we are*
sei *you are*	**siete** *you (all) are*
è *he/she/it is*	**sono** *they are*

Dare, Stare, Andare

Even though some forms are irregular, the **noi** and **voi** forms are often regular because they are not used as frequently. The endings of these irregular verbs show a certain relationship to the regular **-are** present tense endings. Be sure to memorize all irregular verbs.

	dare *to give*	**stare** *to be*	**andare** *to go*
io	**do**	**sto**	**vado**
tu	**dai**	**stai**	**vai**
lui/lei	**dà** (note accent)	**sta**	**va**
noi	**diamo**	**stiamo**	**andiamo**
voi	**date**	**state**	**andate**
loro	**danno**	**stanno**	**vanno**

Fare, Sapere

Sometimes letters appear in the conjugated verb forms that do not appear in the infinitive. **Fare** is actually an irregular infinitive; its obsolete Latin form was *facĕre*. As we have seen above, these two irregular verbs also double the **-n-** in the **loro** form.

	fare *to do, to make*	**sapere** *to know a fact*
io	**faccio**	**so**
tu	**fai**	**sai**
lui/lei	**fa**	**sa**
noi	**facciamo**	**sappiamo**
voi	**fate**	**sapete**
loro	**fanno**	**sanno**

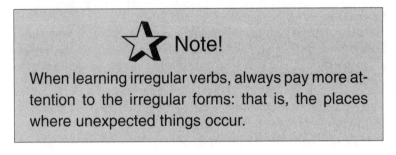

Note!

When learning irregular verbs, always pay more attention to the irregular forms: that is, the places where unexpected things occur.

Bere, Dire

Like **fare**, **bere** and **dire** have irregular infinitives. Their irregular forms maintain letters from the old spellings *bevere* and *dīcĕre*.

	bere *to drink*	**dire** *to say*
io	**bevo**	**dico**
tu	**bevi**	**dici**
lui/lei	**beve**	**dice**
noi	**beviamo**	**diciamo**
voi	**bevete**	**dite**
loro	**bevono**	**dicono**

Verbs with Prefixes

Many important verbs, whether regular or irregular, take on new meanings when a prefix is added. When this happens, the verb with a prefix will conjugate its ending in the same way as the verb from which it was formed. **Contraddire** (*to contradict*), **disdire** (*to retract*), **indire** (*to announce publicly*), **interdire** (*to prohibit*), and **maledire** (*to curse*) are all conjugated like **dire**.

Infinitive: **contraddire**	**disdire**	**interdire**
contraddico	**disdico**	**interdico**
contraddici	**disdici**	**interdici**
contraddice	**disdice**	**interdice**
contraddiciamo	**disdiciamo**	**interdiciamo**
contraddite	**disdite**	**interdite**
contraddicono	**disdicono**	**interdicono**

Verbs Like *tenere* and *venire*

Tenere (*to have, to keep*) and **venire** (*to come*) add a **-g-** to their **io** and
loro present tense forms. In addition, the vowel of the stem changes to
-ie- in the **tu** and **lui/lei** forms. The **noi** and **voi** forms are regular.

Infinitive:	**tenere**	**venire**
io	**tengo**	**vengo**
tu	**tieni**	**vieni**
lui/lei	**tiene**	**viene**
noi	**teniamo**	**veniamo**
voi	**tenete**	**venite**
loro	**tengono**	**vengono**

Verbs like **tenere**	*Verbs like* **venire**
appartenere *to belong*	**avvenire** *to happen*
contenere *to contain*	**convenire** *to convene*
intrattenere *to entertain*	**intervenire** *to intervene*
mantenere *to maintain*	**provenire** *to come from*
sostenere *to support*	**sovvenire** *to help*
trattenere *to detain*	**svenire** *to faint*

✴ **Caution!**

Italian does not use **tenere** (*to have*, in the sense
of *to hold on to, retain*) nearly as much as Spanish.
In daily usage, Italian uses **avere** to mean *to have*.

Sedere

Another verb that changes its vowel to **-ie-** in the present tense stem is
sedere (*to sit*); however, this stem change appears in all forms except **noi**
and **voi**: **siedo, siedi, siede, sediamo, sedete, siedono**. It also has two alternate forms with **gg**: (**io**) **seggo** and (**loro**) **seggono**.

Verbs Ending in -rre

There are three groups of verbs that end in **-rre**. The vowel that precedes the doubled **r** will indicate which set of endings to use in forming the present indicative of these verbs.

Infinitives Ending in -durre

Verbs such as **tradurre** (*to translate*) and **produrre** (*to produce*) once had longer forms in Latin: *tradūcĕre, prodūcĕre*. The stems for the modern present indicative come from these obsolete forms. Once this stem is known, the endings are the same as for regular **-ere** verbs.

Infinitive:	**produrre**	**tradurre**
Stem:	**produc-**	**traduc-**
io	**produco**	**traduco**
tu	**produci**	**traduci**
lui/lei	**produce**	**traduce**
noi	**produciamo**	**traduciamo**
voi	**producete**	**traducete**
loro	**producono**	**traducono**

Other verbs in **-durre** that are conjugated this way are: **introdurre** (*to introduce*), **ridurre** (*to reduce*), and **condurre** (*to lead, conduct*).

Infinitives Ending in -porre

Porre (*to put, to place*) comes from Latin *ponĕre* from which it gets its stem for the present indicative. Note that a **-g-** is added to the stem for **io** and **loro** before the ending is attached. Other verbs that are conjugated the same way are **comporre** (*to compose*), **disporre** (*to dispose, to provide*), **esporre** (*to expose*), **imporre** (*to impose*), **opporre** (*to oppose*), **proporre** (*to propose*), and **supporre** (*to suppose*). Asterisks indicate irregular forms.

Infinitive:	**porre**	**comporre**
Stem:	**pon-**	**compon-**
io	**pongo***	**compongo***
tu	**poni**	**componi**
lui/lei	**pone**	**compone**
noi	**poniamo**	**componiamo**
voi	**ponete**	**componete**
loro	**pongono***	**compongono***

Infinitives Ending in -*trarre*
The verb **trarre** (*to extract, to draw out*) and all verbs formed by adding a prefix to **trarre** have a double **g** in the **io** and **loro** forms. The other forms are based on the original Latin *trahĕre*. Since **h** is always silent in Italian, it has dropped out of the modern stem. Other similar verbs are: **attrarre** (*to attract*), **distrarre** (*to distract*), **contrarre** (*to contract*), and **sottrarre** (*to subtract*). Asterisks indicate irregular forms.

Infinitive:	**trarre**	**attrarre**
Stem:	**tra-**	**attra-**
io	**traggo***	**attraggo***
tu	**trai**	**attrai**
lui/lei	**trae**	**attrae**
noi	**traiamo**	**attraiamo**
voi	**traete**	**attraete**
loro	**traggono***	**attraggono***

Other Irregular Verbs in the Present

Verbs Ending in -*gliere*
Verbs like **cogliere** (*to pick, to gather*) change to **-lg-** in the **io** and **loro** forms: **colgo, cogli, coglie, cogliamo, cogliete, colgono**. Other verbs like this are **accogliere** (*to welcome*), **raccogliere** (*to collect*), and **togliere** (*to remove*).

Parere
The irregular verb **parere** (*to seem*) and other verbs formed by adding a prefix to it form the present tense like this: **paio, pari, pare, paiamo** (OR **pariamo**), **parete, paiono**.

Morire
The verb **morire** (*to die*) also adds an **-i-** to the **io** and **loro** stems. A **-u-** is added to all forms except **noi** and **voi**: **muoio, muori, muore, moriamo, morite, muoiono**.

Udire
The initial vowel in **udire** (*to hear*) changes to **-o-** in all present tense forms except **noi** and **voi**: **odo, odi, ode, udiamo, udite, odono**.

Uscire

The vowel **u** in **uscire** (*to exit, to go out socially*) changes to **e-** in all forms of the present indicative except **noi** and **voi**. The verb **riuscire** (*to succeed at doing something*) is conjugated the same way.

Infinitive:	uscire	riuscire
Irregular stem:	esc-	riesc-
io	esco	riesco
tu	esci	riesci
lui/lei	esce	riesce
noi	usciamo	riusciamo
voi	uscite	riuscite
loro	escono	riescono

Modal Verbs in the Present Tense

Three verbs are frequently used with the infinitive of another verb to modify its meaning: **volere** (*to want to*), **potere** (*to be able to*), and **dovere** (*to have to*). These three have irregularities in several tenses and should be memorized since they are so often used.

Infinitive:	volere	potere	dovere
io	voglio	posso	devo
tu	vuoi	puoi	devi
lui/lei	vuole	può	deve
noi	vogliamo	possiamo	dobbiamo
voi	volete	potete	dovete
loro	vogliono	possono	devono

Vuoi uscire con me? *Do you want to go out with me?*
Posso aiutare? *May I help?*
Dobbiamo pulire la casa. *We must clean the house.*

Imperfect Indicative (*Imperfetto Indicativo*)

The imperfect indicative is used to express a recurrent (habitual, regularly repeated) or ongoing (continuing) action in the past. It is also the only tense used to indicate age, time, size, color, and other descriptions of mental and physical states in the past. Whereas English requires two or more words to indicate this (*I was doing something; we used to do something*), Italian conveys all this information in a single verb form.

Regular Verbs in the Imperfect

For most verbs, the imperfect stem is formed by dropping only the **-re** from the infinitive and adding the endings: **-vo, -vi, -va, -vamo, -vate, -vano**. The examples below show all three conjugations. Notice that in the imperfect, the infix **-isc-** is never used.

Infinitive:	**suonare**	**mettere**	**finire**
Stem:	**suona-**	**mette-**	**fini-**
io	**suonavo**	**mettevo**	**finivo**
tu	**suonavi**	**mettevi**	**finivi**
lui/lei	**suonava**	**metteva**	**finiva**
noi	**suonavamo**	**mettevamo**	**finivamo**
voi	**suonavate**	**mettevate**	**finivate**
loro	**suonavano**	**mettevano**	**finivano**

Suonavo la tromba, ma non lo faccio più. (habitual)
I used to play the trumpet, but I don't do it anymore.
Mamma metteva la frutta nel frigo. (ongoing)
Mom was putting the fruit in the fridge.
Finivano il lavoro alle 17.00; adesso lavorano fino alle 18.00.
(habitual) *They used to finish work at 5 p.m.; now they work until six.*

Irregular Verbs in the Imperfect

There are only a few irregular verbs in the imperfect tense. **Essere** is highly irregular, but very frequently used so it must be memorized. Other irregular verbs maintain obsolete spellings in their imperfect stem, as we have seen happens in the present tense.

Essere

io	**ero**	*I was, I used to be*
tu	**eri**	*you were, you used to be*

lui/lei	era	*he/she/it was, he/she/it used to be*
Lei		*you* (formal) *were, you used to be*
noi	eravamo	*we were, we used to be*
voi	eravate	*you (all) were, you used to be*
loro	erano	*they were, they used to be*
Loro		*you* (formal) *were, you used to be*

Infinitive:	**fare**	**dire**	**bere**	**produrre**	**porre**
Latin					
Infinitive:	*facĕre*	*dīcĕre*	*bevere*	*prodūcĕre*	*ponĕre*
Imperfect					
Stem:	**fac-**	**dic-**	**bev-**	**produc-**	**pon-**
io	**facevo**	**dicevo**	**bevevo**	**producevo**	**ponevo**
tu	**facevi**	**dicevi**	**bevevi**	**producevi**	**ponevi**
lui/lei	**faceva**	**diceva**	**beveva**	**produceva**	**poneva**
noi	**facevamo**	**dicevamo**	**bevevamo**	**producevamo**	**ponevamo**
voi	**facevate**	**dicevate**	**bevevate**	**producevate**	**ponevate**
loro	**facevano**	**dicevano**	**bevevano**	**producevano**	**ponevano**

Trarre
The irregular stem for the imperfect indicative of **trarre** (*to extract, to draw out*) is **tra-**. As with **-ere** verbs, the **-e** from the infinitive is retained in the stem before adding the usual imperfect endings. All verbs ending in **-trarre** follow this pattern: **traevo, traevi, traeva, traevamo, traevate, traevano**.

Uses of the Imperfect Indicative Tense

Italian uses the imperfect much more than English does. Since the word imperfect really means *not perfected*, i.e., not completed, this tense is used to describe continuing, ongoing actions in the past. These may be habitual, regularly done, or recurrent. Frequently, adverbial expressions are used in the same sentence to indicate the ongoing or recurrent nature of the action. These require the use of the imperfect.

> **a volte** *at times*
> **certe volte, qualche volta** *sometimes*
> **continuamente** *continuously*
> **di solito** *usually*

di tanto in tanto *from time to time*
frequentemente *frequently*
il lunedì, la domenica, etc. *on Mondays, on Sundays . . .*
mentre *while*
ogni (giorno, mese, settimana, anno, estate, inverno, etc.)
 every (day, month, week, year, summer, winter, etc.)
sempre *always*
spesso *often*
tutti i giorni *every day*

Da piccola, <u>andava</u> spesso a trovare i nonni.
As a little girl, she used to go visit her grandparents often.
<u>Andavano</u> alla spiaggia ogni estate.
They used to go to the beach every summer.

Remember

English frequently uses *would* to indicate recurrent, habitual actions in the past:

As a little girl, she <u>would</u> often go visit her grandparents.
They <u>would</u> go to the beach every summer.

This must not be confused with the conditional mood in Italian (*would, should, could*). Italian has different verb endings to express *used to* versus *would*.

Simultaneous Actions in the Past
When describing two or more past actions that were going on at the same time, both verbs are conjugated in the imperfect tense.

Io dormivo e Luigi studiava.
I was sleeping and Louis was studying.
Tu parlavi al telefono mentre Anna cucinava.
You were talking on the phone while Ann was cooking.

Physical Description in the Past

Since physical attributes are ongoing and do not suddenly change, the imperfect tense is used to describe physical appearance (height, weight, age, clothing worn, color, etc.)

L'uomo era alto, biondo, e robusto.
The man was tall, blonde, and robust.
Portava una giacca nera.
He was wearing a black jacket.
Il mare era sempre blu.
The sea was always blue.

Description of Mental States and Activities

Since it is hard to determine precisely when emotional and mental states and activities begin or end, these are typically expressed in the imperfect.

Anni fa preferivi andare in montagna.
Years ago you used to prefer going to the mountains.
Sognavamo di viaggiare in Italia.
We used to dream of traveling in Italy.
Giovanna era sempre un po' triste.
Joann was always a bit sad.

The following are verbs that express mental activities. When these were ongoing or repeated in the past, or ongoing but not yet completed or fulfilled, the imperfect must be used. If the action and its consequences are completed, a compound tense will be used.

amare *to love*	**potere** *to be able*
capire *to understand*	**preferire** *to prefer*
credere *to believe*	**sapere** *to know a fact*
desiderare *to desire, to want*	**sperare** *to hope*
odiare *to hate*	**temere** *to fear*
pensare *to think*	**volere** *to want*

You Need to Know ✔

It is difficult to present hard-and-fast rules for choosing which tense to use because, depending on the context, a verb may be used in more than one tense. Later in this chapter you will learn compound (two-part) or "perfect" tenses that are used to show completed actions. For now, be aware that small differences in meaning can be very important in choosing a tense. Compare the models in English below:

Past Action	Implied meaning	Tense Choice
She always hoped to travel	(and never did).	**Imperfect**
She (had) always hoped to travel	(and finally did so).	**Perfect**
He wanted to buy a Ferrari	(but hadn't yet).	**Imperfect**
He (had) wanted to buy a Ferrari	(and did so).	**Perfect**

Time and Weather in the Past

Descriptions concerning the time (hour) in the past are always given using the imperfect tense. The imperfect is also used to refer to the ongoing nature of the weather in a past descriptive context: *It was raining when we left*. One may also use a perfect tense if the atmospheric conditions are entirely completed: *Yesterday it rained. It snowed a lot last January.*

> **Che ora era?** *What time was it?*
> **Erano le tre del pomeriggio.** *It was three in the afternoon.*

Faceva bel tempo in maggio. *It was nice weather in May.*
Pioveva. *It was raining.* (ongoing)
Nevicava. *It was snowing.* (ongoing)
Tirava vento. = **C'era vento.** *It was windy.* (ongoing)

Preterit Tense (*Passato Remoto*)

Regular Preterit Verbs

The preterit (also called the past absolute or past definite) expresses the completion of an action or a state of being in the remote past, a distant temporal period that no longer has a direct relation to the present.

Regular verbs form the preterit stem by dropping the **-re** from the infinitive. The "characteristic vowel" (**-a-**, **-e-**, **-i-**) of each conjugation is retained in the stem except for the **lui/lei** form where this vowel drops. In each conjugation the **lui/lei** form is accented, but the vowel of the ending differs. All regular **io** forms end in two vowels. As with the imperfect, there is no **-isc-** used with **-ire** verbs.

Infinitive:	**parlare**	**credere**	**finire**
Stem:	**parla-**	**crede-**	**fini-**
io	**parlai**	**credei**	**finii**
tu	**parlasti**	**credesti**	**finisti**
lui/lei	**parlò**	**credé**	**finì**
noi	**parlammo**	**credemmo**	**finimmo**
voi	**parlaste**	**credeste**	**finiste**
loro	**parlarono**	**crederono**	**finirono**

Allowing for the spelling adjustments noted above, the regular preterit endings are: **-i, -sti, an accented single vowel, -mmo, -ste, -rono**. These have a certain, rough relationship to the present tense endings (**tu** ends in **-i**, **noi** ends in **-mo**, **voi** ends in **-te**, **loro** has a final **-no**), but with additional elements and other small variations.

In addition to these regular preterit endings, a group of second conjugation verbs has alternate endings for the **io**, **lui/lei**, and **loro** forms. (See the forms in parentheses below.) These endings incorporate a double **t** and descend from medieval western Tuscan usage. As is often the case in Italian, either version is permissible. Here are two examples:

	credere *(to believe)*	**ricevere** *(to receive)*
io	**credei (credetti)**	**ricevei (ricevetti)**
tu	credesti	ricevesti
lui/lei	**credé (credette)**	**ricevé (ricevette)**
noi	credemmo	ricevemmo
voi	credeste	riceveste
loro	**crederono (credettero)**	**riceverono (ricevettero)**

Irregular Preterit ("1–3–3") Verbs

Many verbs are irregular in the preterit, especially those of the second conjugation (**-ere** verbs). Some verbs have two different stems in the preterit: one that is regular (like the spelling of the infinitive) and one that is highly irregular and must be memorized. Such verbs are irregular in the <u>first</u> and <u>third</u> persons singular (**io, lui/lei**) and in the <u>third</u> person plural (**loro**), giving rise to the nickname "1–3–3" verbs. This group of verbs has its own set of endings that bears a certain relationship to the regular preterit endings: **-i, -sti, -e (no accent), -mmo, -ste, -ero**. Observe which forms have regular or irregular stems in the charts below:

Infinitive: **chiudere** *(to close)*

	Regular Stem: **chiud-**	*Irregular Stem:* **chius-**
io	—	**chiusi**
tu	**chiudesti**	—
lui/lei	—	**chiuse**
noi	**chiudemmo**	—
voi	**chiudeste**	—
loro	—	**chiusero**

Infinitive: **rimanere** *(to remain)*

	Regular Stem: **rimane-**	*Irregular Stem:* **rimas-**
io	—	**rimasi**
tu	**rimanesti**	—
lui/lei	—	**rimase**
noi	**rimanemmo**	—
voi	**rimaneste**	—
loro	—	**rimasero**

Other verbs that have a single **s** in the irregular preterit stem are listed below. Only the first three persons are given in the chart: **loro** uses the same irregular stem as **io** and **lei**; the stem for **tu**, **noi**, and **voi** follows the spelling of the infinitive.

chiedere *to ask*	**chiesi, chiedesti, chiese**, . . .
concludere *to conclude*	**conclusi, concludesti, concluse**, . . .
decidere *to decide*	**decisi, decidesti, decise**, . . .
dividere *to divide*	**divisi, dividesti, divise**, . . .
prendere *to take*	**presi, prendesti, prese**, . . .
ridere *to laugh*	**risi, ridesti, rise**, . . .
rispondere *to answer*	**risposi, rispondesti, rispose**, . . .
mettere *to put, to place*	**misi, mettesti, mise**, . . .
porre *to put, to position*	**posi, ponesti, posi**, . . .

As we have seen, when a prefix is added to a verb, the new verb conjugates in the same way. **Sorridere** works like **ridere**; **accludere, escludere, includere** work like **concludere**; **coincidere** and **uccidere** work like **decidere**. Other verbs conjugated like **prendere** are: **accendere, apprendere, attendere, difendere, offendere, scendere, sorprendere, spendere, stendere**. Some verbs like **mettere** are: **ammettere, commettere, permettere, promettere, rimettere, smettere, trasmettere**. Verbs like **porre** are: **comporre, disporre, opporre, preporre, proporre**.

All these irregular preterits from **-ere** verbs had a single **s** in their irregular stem. Another group of 1–3–3 verbs has a double **ss** in their irregular stem and also loses a letter or two from the normal stem. Study the examples below; the forms with irregular stems are in bold.

	leggere (*to read*)	**scrivere** (*to write*)	**vivere** (*to live*)
io	**lessi**	**scrissi**	**vissi**
tu	leggesti	scrivesti	vivesti
lui/lei	**lesse**	**scrisse**	**visse**
noi	leggemmo	scrivemmo	vivemmo
voi	leggeste	scriveste	viveste
loro	**lessero**	**scrissero**	**vissero**

Again, if a prefix is added to one of these verbs, the new verb will be conjugated in the same way. Verbs conjugated like **leggere** include:

correggere, eleggere, proteggere, reggere. Other verbs like **scrivere** are: **descrivere, iscrivere, prescrivere, trascrivere**, etc.

Verbs ending in **-durre** (**produrre, addurre, condurre, introdurre, tradurre**, etc.) and **dire** (**contraddire, disdire, maledire, ridire**, etc.) also have a double s in the **io**, **lui/lei**, and **loro** forms of the preterit. Verbs like **trarre** also have a double s, but the **-e-** from the normal stem is dropped in the irregular stem.

	produrre	**dire**	**trarre**
io	**produssi**	**dissi**	**trassi**
tu	producesti	dicesti	traesti
lui/lei	**produsse**	**disse**	**trasse**
noi	producemmo	dicemmo	traemmo
voi	produceste	diceste	traeste
loro	**produssero**	**dissero**	**trassero**

Not all irregular preterit verbs of the 1–3–3 type have **-s-** or **-ss-** in their irregular stems. Some verbs have another consonant + s. Many have doubled consonants that derive from the spelling of their infinitive. Here are more examples of irregular preterits followed by lists of similar verbs that form their preterit in the same way.

correre *(to run)*: corsi, corresti, corse, corremmo, correste, corsero

Also, **occorrere, incorrere, precorrere, rincorrere, scorrere, trascorrere**.

scegliere *(to choose)*: scelsi, scegliesti, scelse, scegliemmo, sceglieste, scelsero

Also, **accogliere, cogliere, raccogliere, togliere**.

volgere *(to turn)*: volsi, volgesti, volse, volgemmo, volgeste, volsero

Also, **dipingere, fingere, giungere, piangere, scorgere, sorgere, spingere, svolgere**.

cadere *(to fall)*: caddi, cadesti, cadde, cademmo, cadeste, caddero

Also, **decadere, ricadere**.

tenere *(to hold, keep)*: tenni, tenesti, tenne, tenemmo, teneste, tennero

Also, **appartenere, contenere, mantenere, sostenere**.

volere *(to want)*: volli, volesti, volle, volemmo, voleste, vollero

bere *(to drink)*: bevvi, bevesti, bevve, bevemmo, beveste, bevvero

fare *(to do, to make)*: feci, facesti, fece, facemmo, faceste, fecero
        Also, **contraffare, disfare, rifare, soddisfare, sopraffare**.

dare *(to give):* diedi (detti), desti, diede (dette), demmo, deste, diedero (dettero)

stare *(to stay; to be [for health])*: stetti, stesti, stette, stemmo, steste, stettero

vedere *(to see)*: vidi, vedesti, vide, vedemmo, vedeste, videro
        Also, **intravedere, prevedere, provvedere, rivedere**.

venire *(to come)*: venni, venisti, venne, venimmo, veniste, vennero
        Also, **avvenire, convenire, divenire, intervenire, pervenire, rivenire, sopravvenire, sovvenire, svenire**.

conoscere *(to be acquainted with)*: conobbi, conoscesti, conobbe, conoscemmo, conosceste, conobbero
        Also, **riconoscere**.

nascere *(to be born)*: nacqui, nascesti, nacque, nascemmo, nasceste, nacquero

piacere *(to please)*: piacqui, piacesti, piacque, piacemmo, piaceste, piacquero

rompere *(to break)*: ruppi, rompesti, ruppe, rompemmo, rompeste, ruppero

sapere *(to know a fact)*: seppi, sapesti, seppe, sapemmo, sapeste, seppero

Uses of the Preterit

The preterit expresses the completion of an action or state of being in the past without any relation to the present. This tense is used frequently in narrative literature, but it is not only a literary tense: in Sicily the preterit is still used in daily conversation to indicate past completed actions that are not remote.

    The preterit must be used to describe historic events or in biographies of famous people now dead. The following are some common expressions that would indicate an action completed in the distant past:

l'anno scorso *last year*
l'estate scorsa *last summer*
l'inverno scorso *last winter*
dieci anni fa *ten years ago*
nell'autunno del 1952 *in the autumn of 1952*
nel 1492 *in 1492*

Here are some examples of past events described using the preterit.

Dante Alighieri morí nel 1321.
Dante Alighieri died in 1321.
I miei nonni vennero in America nel 1911.
My grandparents came to America in 1911.
Mio padre incontrò mia madre nel 1948.
My father met my mother in 1948.
Nacqui nel 1954.
I was born in 1954.

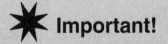

✸ Important!

The more tenses you learn and want to use, the more important it is to write and pronounce the conjugated forms correctly. Observe how details such as missed accents or mispronounced vowels change the meaning of a verb form:
parlo *I speak* BUT: **parlò** *he/she spoke*
credesti *you* (sing.) *believed*
                    BUT: **credeste** *you* (plur.) *believed*

The Future Tense (*Futuro semplice*)

As we have seen, the present indicative can be used to indicate future actions in both English and Italian: **Quest'estate vado a Roma.** *(This sum-*

mer I am going to Rome.) In both sentences, the action has not yet taken place.

Italian does have a special set of stems and endings to form the simple (one-part) future tense. These clearly indicate an action that will happen: **Quest'estate andrò a Roma**. (*This summer I will go to Rome.*) The future tense always translates as "will do something."

To form the simple future tense, the final **e** is dropped from the infinitive of all three conjugations. A vowel and the **-r-** remain, producing a longer stem than for the present indiciative. For reasons of pronunciation, the **a** in **-are** verbs changes to **e** in the future stem. In the future tense, there is only one set of endings for all verbs, regular or irregular: **-ò, -ai, à, -emo, -ete, -anno**. The infix **-isc-** is never used in the future tense. Pay special attention to the grave accents and the double **n** in the **loro** form. These must always be observed.

Regular Verbs in the Future

Infinitive:	**suonare**	**mettere**	**finire**
Future Stem:	**suoner-**	**metter-**	**finir-**
io	**suonerò**	**metterò**	**finirò**
tu	**suonerai**	**metterai**	**finirai**
lui/lei	**suonerà**	**metterà**	**finirà**
noi	**suoneremo**	**metteremo**	**finiremo**
voi	**suonerete**	**metterete**	**finirete**
loro	**suoneranno**	**metteranno**	**finiranno**

We have seen elsewhere that endings with **c** or **g** must be adjusted to maintain the hard or soft sound of the original word. Verb with infinitives ending in **-ciare** and **-giare** drop the **i** before adding the future endings to their stems:

Infinitive:	**cominciare**	**viaggiare**
Future Stem:	**comincer-**	**viagger-**
io	**comincerò**	**viaggerò**
tu	**comincerai**	**viaggerai**
lui/lei	**comincerà**	**viaggerà**
noi	**cominceremo**	**viaggeremo**
voi	**comincerete**	**viaggerete**
loro	**cominceranno**	**viaggeranno**

Verbs with infinitives ending in **-care** and **-gare** must add an **h** to their future tense stems:

Infinitive:	**cercare**	**pagare**
Future Stem:	**cercher-**	**pagher-**
io	**cercherò**	**pagherò**
tu	**cercherai**	**pagherai**
lui/lei	**cercherà**	**pagherà**
noi	**cercheremo**	**pagheremo**
voi	**cercherete**	**pagherete**
loro	**cercheranno**	**pagheranno**

Irregular Verbs in the Future

Many common verbs have irregular future stems. Short infinitives like **dare**, **fare**, and **stare** simply drop the final **e** before adding future tense endings. Many **-ere** verbs lose the internal **-e-** and have a shortened stem with two different adjacent consonants. Other verbs, often of the second and third conjugations, drop their final **e** and have double consonants in their future stem. All forms of **essere** are irregular. Fortunately, the future tense endings are always the same, even for the verbs with irregular stems.

Infinitive	*Stem*	*Future Tense Forms*
andare	*andr-*	**andrò, andrai, andrà, andremo, andrete, andranno**
avere	*avr-*	**avrò, avrai, avrà, avremo, avrete, avranno**
bere	*berr-*	**berrò, berrai, berrà, berremo, berrete, berranno**
cadere	*cadr-*	**cadrò, cadrai, cadrà, cadremo, cadrete, cadranno**
dare	*dar-*	**darò, darai, darà, daremo, darete, daranno**
fare	*far-*	**farò, farai, farà, faremo, farete, faranno**
stare	*star-*	**starò, starai, starà, staremo, starete, staranno**
essere	*sar-*	**sarò, sarai, sarà, saremo, sarete, saranno**
dovere	*dovr-*	**dovrò, dovrai, dovrà, dovremo, dovrete, dovranno**
potere	*potr-*	**potrò, potrai, potrà, potremo, potrete, potranno**
volere	*vorr-*	**vorrò, vorrai, vorrà, vorremo, vorrete, vorranno**
sapere	*sapr-*	**saprò, saprai, saprà, sapremo, saprete, sapranno**
vedere	*vedr-*	**vedrò, vedrai, vedrà, vedremo, vedrete, vedranno**
venire	*verr-*	**verrò, verrai, verrà, verremo, verrete, verranno**
vivere	*vivr-*	**vivrò, vivrai, vivrà, vivremo, vivrete, vivranno**

Be careful not to confuse the stems for **venire** (**verr-**) and **volere** (**vorr-**): they both have double **r**. Look carefully at the vowel of the stem to that of the infinitive to match meanings.

Hint!

Memorize the irregular future tense stems well. The same stems are used to form the conditional present mood of these verbs.

Special Uses of the Future

The Future of Probability
In Italian, the future tense may be used to express probability or possibility in the present. This is typically used for suppositions in questions or answers when the precise information sought is not definitely known.

> **Dove <u>sarà</u> Pietro?**
> *Where can Peter be?*
> **<u>Sarà</u> a casa. <u>Starà</u> male.**
> *He's probably at home. He might be sick.*

> **Quanti anni <u>avrà</u> il professore?**
> *How old can the professor be?*
> **<u>Avrà</u> sessant'anni.**
> *He must be about sixty years old.*

The Future after *quando* and *se*
Also unlike English, when **quando** (*when*) and **se** (*if*) indicate a future action, Italian uses the future for the verbs in both clauses. English mixes present and future. Observe:

> **Quando arriveranno, discuteremo il problema.** (Fut./Fut.)
> *When they arrive, we will discuss the problem.* (Pres./Fut.)

Se farà cattivo tempo, resteremo a casa. (Fut./Fut.)
If the weather is bad, we'll stay home. (Pres./Fut.)

The Conditional Mood

In Italian, as in English, verbs in the present conditional express the notion *would do something* if a certain condition is obtained. The conditional stems for all Italian verbs are identical to the future tense stems (see above). The conditional adds its own set of endings: **-ei, -esti, -ebbe, -emmo, -este, -ero**. These bear a distinct resemblance to various preterit endings. Unlike the future, there are no accented endings in the conditional. Here are some examples of verbs in the conditional followed by sample sentences.

Infinitive	*Stem*	*Present Conditional Forms*
avere	*avr-*	**avrei, avresti, avrebbe, avremmo, avreste, avrebbero**
cercare	*cercher-*	**cercherei, cercheresti, cercherebbe, cercheremmo, cerchereste, cercherebbero**
dare	*dar-*	**darei, daresti, darebbe, daremmo, dareste, darebbero**
dovere	*dovr-*	**dovrei, dovresti, dovrebbe, dovremmo, dovreste, dovrebbero**
essere	*sar-*	**sarei, saresti, sarebbe, saremmo, sareste, sarebbero**
potere	*potr-*	**potrei, potresti, potrebbe, potremmo, potreste, potrebbero**
volere	*vorr-*	**vorrei, vorresti, vorrebbe, vorremmo, vorreste, vorrebbero**

<u>Darebbero</u> molti soldi ai poveri.
They would give a lot of money to the poor.
<u>Cercheremmo</u> un libro interessante in biblioteca.
We would look for (seek) an interesting book in the library.
<u>Sarebbe</u> molto strano portare quel vestito alla festa.
It would be very strange to wear that suit to the party.

Modal Verbs in the Present Conditional
Any verb conjugated in the present conditional gives the meaning *would do something*. To add particular emotional spins to a verb (*should, could,*

would like), helper verbs called modal verbs must be used: **dovere**, **potere**, **volere**. These are conjugated by using the conditional stem and endings, but the verb they accompany remains as an infinitive (unconjugated). These are used very frequently in daily conversation, writing, and literature.

> conditional of **dovere** + infinitive = *should* do something
> conditional of **potere** + infinitive = *could* do something
> conditional of **volere** + infinitive = *would like to* do something

> **Giovanni <u>dovrebbe</u> uscire, ma deve studiare**.
> *John would like to go out, but he has to study.*
> **<u>Potremmo</u> andare al cinema**.
> *We could go to the movies.*
> **<u>Vorrei</u> comprare una bella casa in campagna**.
> *I would like to buy a lovely house in the country.*

Compound Tenses

The Present Perfect Tense (*Passato Prossimo*)

All the tenses you have studied so far in this book have been "simple tenses." In such tenses there is only one part to the verb, and it tells three things: who did the action, the nature of the action, and when the action is or was done. Let's analyze the components of the single verb form **guarderai** (*you will watch*). The root **guard-** indicates the action of watching; the stem **guarder-** indicates the action will be done in the future; and the ending **-ai** identifies *you* (familiar) as the doer of the action.

Now you will learn compound or "perfect" tenses. These always indicate a completed (thoroughly done) action. In these, two parts to the verb are needed to convey all this information: doer, action, time frame. Compound tenses are formed by conjugating the auxiliary verb, either **avere** or **essere**, and placing it before a past participle. The past participle is equivalent to using **-ed** in English.

Regular past participles are formed by dropping the **-are**, **-ere**, or **-ire** from an infinitive and adding, respectively, **-ato**, **-uto**, **-ito**.

First Conjugation	*Second Conjugation*	*Third Conjugation*
ballare → **ballato**	**avere** → **avuto**	**capire** → **capito**
cantare → **cantato**	**sapere** → **saputo**	**finire** → **finito**
mangiare → **mangiato**	**vendere** → **venduto**	**vestire** → **vestito**

Note that the participle only describes the action and tells that it is completed. To show the doer of the action, the auxiliary (**avere** or **essere**) must be used. To form the present perfect tense, use the present tense forms of the auxiliary plus the past participle.

Regular First Conjugation: **ballare**

io	**ho ballato**	*I danced (I did dance)*
tu	**hai ballato**	*you danced (you did dance)*
lui/lei	**ha ballato**	*he/she/it danced (he/she did dance)*
Lei		*you* (formal) *danced*
noi	**abbiamo ballato**	*we danced (we did dance)*
voi	**avete ballato**	*you (all) danced (you did dance)*
loro }	**hanno ballato**	*they danced (they did dance)*
Loro		*you* (pl. formal) *danced*

Regular Second Conjugation: **vendere**

io	**ho venduto**	*I sold (I did sell)*
tu	**hai venduto**	*you sold (you did sell)*
lui/lei	**ha venduto**	*he/she sold (did sell)*
noi	**abbiamo venduto**	*we sold (did sell)*
voi	**avete venduto**	*you (all) sold (did sell)*
loro	**hanno venduto**	*they sold (did sell)*

Regular Third Conjugation: **finire**

io	**ho finito**	*I finished (did finish)*
tu	**hai finito**	*you finished (did finish, etc.)*
lui/lei	**ha finito**	*he/she/it finished*
noi	**abbiamo finito**	*we finished*
voi	**avete finito**	*you (all) finished*
loro	**hanno finito**	*they finished*

Hint!

Since the simple tense forms of **avere** and **essere** are used to form various compound tenses, it is a good idea to memorize all their simple tense forms well before learning other verbs. **Avere** and **essere** are needed frequently in many tenses.

Irregular Past Participles

Many verbs in Italian have irregular past participles. Here is a list of common verbs that take **avere** in the present perfect with their irregular participles. As you learn these, be aware that several spelling patterns recur: **-erto, -lto, -nto, -rso, -so, -sso, -sto, -tto**. Occasionally an irregular **-ere** verb forms its past participle with **-ito** (**assistere** → **assistito**), as do some **-ire** verbs that form theirs with **-uto** (**venire** → **venuto**).

Infinitive	*Past Participle*
-erto	
aprire (*to open*)	**aperto**
coprire (*to cover*)	**coperto**
offrire (*to offer*)	**offerto**
soffrire (*to suffer*)	**sofferto**
-lto	
cogliere (*to gather*)	**colto**
scegliere (*to select*)	**scelto**
volgere (*to turn*)	**volto**
-nto	
piangere (*to cry*)	**pianto**
vincere (*to win*)	**vinto**
-rso	
apparire (*to appear*)	**apparso**
correre (*to run*)	**corso**
perdere (*to lose*)	**perso**

-so

chiudere (*to close*)	**chiuso**
difendere (*to defend*)	**difeso**
dividere (*to divide*)	**diviso**
prendere (*to take*)	**preso**
spendere (*to spend money*)	**speso**
ridere (*to laugh*)	**riso**
uccidere (*to kill*)	**ucciso**

-sso

mettere (*to put*)	**messo**

-sto

chiedere (*to ask, request*)	**chiesto**
rispondere (*to respond*)	**risposto**
porre (*to put, position*)	**posto**

-tto

cuocere (*to cook*)	**cotto**
dire (*to say*)	**detto**
fare (*to do, to make*)	**fatto**
leggere (*to read*)	**letto**
rompere (*to break*)	**rotto**
scrivere (*to write*)	**scritto**

Remember

Whenever a verb has an added prefix or similar spelling, it will be manipulated like the root verb: **(dis)dire** → **(dis)detto**, **(con)dividere** → **(con)diviso**, **(contraf)fare** → **(contraf)fatto**, etc.

Nouns and Adjectives Formed from Past Participles

Irregular past participles frequently are used as adjectives or with a definite article as nouns (often feminine). If you learn these forms well, it will help in discerning the meaning of the related nouns and adjectives. Here are some examples:

Past Participle	Adjectival Form	Noun Form
aperto	aperto, -a, -i, -e (open)	
chiuso	chiuso, -a, -i, -e (closed)	
corso		il corso (the course)
		la corsa (the race)
cotto	cotto, -a, -i, -e (cooked)	
offerto		l'offerta (the offer)
preso	preso, -a, -i, -e (captured)	la presa (the taking of)
risposto		la risposta (the answer)

Agreement of Past Participle: *Avere* **Verbs**
The term for verbs that take **avere** in compound tenses is transitive verbs. This means that they transfer the action from the subject to a direct object. The action of the verb is incomplete unless there is a direct object, whether explicitly stated or unstated. To decide if a verb is transitive, ask the question *What?* or *Whom?*

> *I ate the pizza.* (*Ask:* "What did I eat?" "The pizza.")

In this sentence "I" is the doer, the action is eating, and "the pizza" is the direct object (what got eaten). Verbs may be transitive in one language, but not in another. To be sure, check a good dictionary which will indicate this by an abbreviation such as "*t.*" or "*trans.*"

If the direct object is replaced by a pronoun (see Chapter 8: Pronouns), the pronoun will be placed before **avere** in a compound tense. When this happens, the ending of the past participle will change to show the agreement with the gender and number of the direct object, much as adjectives do. The direct objects, their pronouns, and agreements are underlined in the following models:

> **Ho comprato i libri.** *I (have) bought the books.*
> **Li ho comprati.** *I (have) bought them.*

> **Hai ricevuto le lettere.** *You (have) received the letters.*
> **Le hai ricevute.** *You (have) received them.*

> **Abbiamo veduto Francesca.** *We have seen (saw) Frances.*
> **L'abbiamo veduta.** *We have seen her.*

The Present Perfect of Verbs Conjugated with *Essere*
Another group of verbs is conjugated in the compound tenses using **essere** plus the past participle. These verbs do not have a direct object; instead, the action is completed by the subject itself. Such verbs usually describe motion from place to place or states of being. Here is a list of common intransitive verbs; these <u>always</u> require **essere**. Asterisks indicate the irregular forms.

andare (*to go*)	**andato**
arrivare (*to arrive*)	**arrivato**
cadere (*to fall*)	**caduto**
crescere (*to grow*)	**cresciuto***
diventare (*to become*)	**diventato**
durare (*to last, endure*)	**durato**
entrare (*to enter*)	**entrato**
essere (*to be*)	**stato***
morire (*to die*)	**morto***
nascere (*to be born*)	**nato***
partire (*to leave, depart*)	**partito**
(ri)tornare (*to return*)	**(ri)tornato**
salire (*to go up, ascend*)	**salito**
scendere (*to descend*)	**sceso***
stare (*to stay, to be for health*)	**stato**
uscire (*to go out*)	**uscito**
venire (*to come*)	**venuto***

Note that the past participle for both **essere** and **stare** is **stato**.

To conjugate an intransitive verb in the present perfect, use the present tense form of **essere** plus the past participle of the verb. Since the action is directly related to the subject and does not transfer to a direct object, the past participle will make an agreement with the subject much as adjectives agree with the nouns they modify. Since each past participle ends in **-o**, each one will have four possible endings when **essere** is used. As with adjective agreements, a group of men, or men and women mixed, will take the masculine plural ending **-i**; a group of entirely women is feminine plural **-e**.

Andare

Io sono andato (-a) *I went*
Tu sei andato (-a) *You went*

Lui è andato *(m. sing.) He went*
Lei è andata *(f. sing.) She went; you (formal) went*
— **è andato (-a)** *It went*
Noi studenti siamo andati *(m. plur.) We students went*
Noi donne siamo andate *(f. plur.) We ladies went*
Voi ragazzi siete andati *(m. plur.) You guys went*
Voi donne siete andate *(f. plur.) You ladies went*
I ragazzi sono andati *(m. plur.) The guys went*
Le ragazze sono andate *(f. plur.) The girls went*

Here are all the possible forms of an **-ere** and an **-ire** verb:

	cadere *(to fall)*	**uscire** *(to go out)*
io	**sono caduto (-a)**	**sono uscito (-a)**
tu	**sei caduto (-a)**	**sei uscito (-a)**
lui	**è caduto**	**è uscito**
lei	**è caduta**	**è uscita**
noi	**siamo caduti (-e)**	**siamo usciti (-e)**
voi	**siete caduti (-e)**	**siete usciti (-e)**
loro	**sono caduti (-e)**	**sono usciti (-e)**

Remember

All past participles of verbs conjugated with **essere** must agree in gender and number with the subject of the sentence:
Il ragazzo è partito dalla casa.
(*m. sing.*)
La ragazza è partita dalla casa.
(*f. sing.*)
I ragazzi sono partiti dalla casa.
(*m. pl.*)
Le ragazze sono partite dalla casa. (*f. pl.*)

The Present Perfect Versus the Imperfect Indicative

The present perfect indicates an action completed in the not-too-distant past. The Italian term **passato prossimo** indicates this: "the past in the vicinity of . . ." or "nearby past."

> **L'altro giorno Alberto ha salutato la maestra.**
> *The other day Albert greeted his teacher.*
> **Sono arrivati ieri.** *They arrived yesterday.*
> **Ho guardato un programma ieri sera.**
> *I watched a program yesterday evening.*

These expressions indicate a recent past time frame:

> **ieri** *yesterday*
> **ieri l'altro, l'altro ieri** *the day before yesterday*
> **ieri mattina** *yesterday morning*
> **ieri pomeriggio** *yesterday afternoon*
> **ieri sera** *yesterday evening, last night*
> **due giorni fa** *two days ago*
> **tre mesi fa** *three months ago*
> **domenica scorsa** *last Sunday*
> **martedì scorso** *last Tuesday*
> **l'anno scorso** *last year*

You will recall that the imperfect describes repeated, habitual, or on-going actions in the past. The **passato prossimo** describes past actions as well, but these are completed. The same verb may be used in either tense, but the meaning will differ.

> **Il sabato la signora puliva la casa.** (habitual)
> *On Saturdays the lady used to clean the house.*
> **L'altro giorno la signora ha pulito la casa.** (once)
> *The other day the lady cleaned the house.*

> **Uscivano insieme l'anno scorso.** (habitual)
> *They used to go out together last year.*
> **Sono usciti insieme venerdì sera.** (once)
> *They went out together Friday night.*

When two or more actions in the past are completed, the **passato prossimo** is used to express this.

> **Ho pulito la casa, ho fatto un panino, e sono uscita.**
> *I cleaned the house, made a sandwich, and left.*
> **Teresa è andata al cinema, ma Luigi è rimasto a casa.**
> *Therese went to the movies, but Louis stayed home.*

A continuing action in the past (imperfect) may be interrupted by a completed, specific action, expressed in the **passato prossimo**.

> **Maria leggeva il giornale quando siamo arrivati.**
> *Mary was reading the newspaper when we arrived.*
> **La nonna dormiva quando il telefono ha squillato.**
> *Grandmother was sleeping when the phone rang.*

Pluperfect Indicative (*Trapassato Prossimo*)

The pluperfect indicative tense (**trapassato prossimo**) is formed by using the imperfect form of **avere** or **essere** plus the past participle. All other rules regarding agreement follow the usage of the **passato prossimo**. The pluperfect indicates an action completed in the past prior to another past action. In the sentence, *I found the money that I had lost*, the second verb (*I had lost*) is in the pluperfect and indicates the antecedent action. Pluperfect verbs in Italian will always translate "had done something." English tends not to say the "had" which may lead to confusion with the present perfect tense. By contrast, Italian always accounts for the precise time frame of an action.

Pluperfect with *avere* Verbs

	parlare	credere	finire
io	avevo parlato	avevo creduto	avevo finito
tu	avevi parlato	avevi creduto	avevi finito
lui/lei	aveva parlato	aveva creduto	aveva finito
noi	avevamo parlato	avevamo creduto	avevamo finito
voi	avevate parlato	avevate creduto	avevate finito
loro	avevano parlato	avevano creduto	avevano finito

Pluperfect with *essere* Verbs

	andare	cadere	uscire
io	ero andato (-a)	ero caduto (-a)	ero uscito (-a)
tu	eri andato (-a)	eri caduto (-a)	eri uscito (-a)
lui	era andato	era caduto	era uscito
lei	era andata	era caduta	era uscita
noi	eravamo andati (-e)	eravamo caduti (-e)	eravamo usciti (-e)
voi	eravate andati (-e)	eravate caduti (-e)	eravate usciti (-e)
loro	erano andati (-e)	erano caduti (-e)	erano usciti (-e)

Erano già **partiti** quando gli ho telefonato.
They had already left when I phoned them.
Avevo appena **chiuso** le finestre quando è cominciato a piovere.
I had just closed the windows when it began to rain.
Ha parlato con la moglie perché il marito non aveva ascoltato.
He (she) spoke with the wife because the husband had not listened.

Preterite Perfect Tense (Trapassato Remoto)

The preterite perfect tense is formed by using the preterit of **avere** or **es-sere** and the past participle of the acting verb. It is used to describe an action completed prior to another in the far distant past, frequently in a literary context. Note that both **avere** and **essere** are irregular in this tense.

	with *avere*	with *essere*
	cantare	arrivare
io	ebbi cantato	fui arrivato (-a)
tu	avesti cantato	fosti arrivato (-a)
lui	ebbe cantato	fu arrivato
lei	ebbe cantato	fu arrivata
noi	avemmo cantato	fummo arrivati (-e)
voi	aveste cantato	foste arrivati (-e)
loro	ebbero cantato	furono arrivati (-e)

Appena fu arrivato, cominciò a parlare.
As soon as he had arrived, he began to speak.
Dopo che ebbero finito di parlare, uscirono di casa.
After they had finished speaking, they went out of the house.

The preterite perfect, used mostly in literary contexts, is always preceded by time expressions such as **appena, non appena** (*as soon as*); **dopo che** (*after*); **quando** (*when*); **come** (*as*); or **finché non** (*until*). The preterite perfect is used in the dependent clause and the preterit (**passato remoto**) will be used in the independent clause.

Future Perfect Tense (*Futuro Anteriore*)

The future perfect tense is formed by using the future of **avere** or **essere** and the past participle of the acting verb. It expresses a future action that will be completed prior to another future action.

	with avere	with essere
	comprare	uscire
io	avrò comprato	sarò uscito (-a)
tu	avrai comprato	sarai uscito (-a)
lui	avrà comprato	sarà uscito
lei	avrà comprato	sarà uscita
noi	avremo comprato	saremo usciti (-e)
voi	avrete comprato	sarete usciti (-e)
loro	avranno comprato	saranno usciti (-e)

Voi <u>sarete</u> già <u>partiti</u> quando noi arriveremo.
You will have already left when we arrive.
<u>Avranno cenato</u> prima di partire.
They will have dined before leaving.

Conditional Perfect Tense (*Condizionale Passato*)

The conditional perfect is formed by using the conditional of **avere** or **essere** and the past participle of the acting verb. It expresses the notion *would have* to describe something that would have taken place had something else not intervened.

	with *avere*	with *essere*
	mangiare	salire
io	avrei mangiato	sarei salito (-a)
tu	avresti mangiato	saresti salito (-a)
lui	avrebbe mangiato	sarebbe salito
lei	avrebbe mangiato	sarebbe salita
noi	avremmo mangiato	saremmo saliti (-e)
voi	avreste mangiato	sareste saliti (-e)
loro	avrebbero mangiato	sarebbero saliti (-e)

<u>Sarebbero venuti</u> ma non avevano abbastanza tempo.
They would have come but they didn't have enough time.
Avevi promesso che <u>avresti scritto</u> spesso.
You had promised that you would have written often.

You Need to Know ✔

The term "perfect" means an action is thoroughly done. All perfect tenses describe specific, completed, one-time actions. The temporal distance from the speaker or narrator (time frame) varies. Different perfect tenses are made by conjugating the auxiliary in different tenses. All the other rules apply as for present perfect.

Present Perfect: **ho parlato** *I have spoken*
Pluperfect: **avevo parlato** *I had spoken*
Preterite Perfect: **ebbi parlato** *I had spoken*
Future Perfect: **avrò parlato** *I will have spoken*
Conditional Perfect: **avrei parlato** *I would have spoken*

The Subjunctive

In Italian and other languages, special verb forms are used in dependent clauses after expressions that shift the sentence's meaning from the realm of factual reality into a less certain area of opinion or possibility. Such sentences have an emotional spin and pertain to belief, doubt, desire, demand, volition, uncertainty, etc. When an action or statement is real and true, the indicative tenses are used. When an action is referred to or a subjective statement is made, the verb in the dependent clause must use a subjunctive form of the verb. Observe the difference in these models:

Indicative (true fact)	Subjunctive (belief, possibility)
Giovanni arriva stasera.	**Credo che Giovanni arrivi stasera.**
John arrives this evening.	*I think that John arrives this evening.*
Vengono da me.	**Voglio che vengano da me.**
They're coming to my place.	*I want them to come to my place.*
Fa caldo fuori.	**Pensate che faccia caldo fuori?**
It's hot outside.	*Do you think that it's hot outside?*

By prefacing even a factual statement with an expression like *I believe, I want, Do you think?* etc., the verb must shift into the subjunctive to show that it is now in the realm of opinion.

In Italian, there are four subjunctive moods that relate to tenses you have already learned: the present subjunctive, the past subjunctive, the imperfect subjunctive, and the pluperfect subjunctive. Their meanings parallel the corresponding indicative tenses. Some of their stems and endings also resemble tenses you already know; others are distinctive and must be memorized. As for any tense, some verbs are regular and others have irregularities. The particular combination of stems and endings allows us to express an opinion, desire, belief, etc., in any time frame, about an action that is occurring or has occurred in any other time frame.

At times English language speakers are confused about the use of the subjunctive. That is because English rarely uses this construction and does not have special verb forms to talk about things in a subjective vein. Examples in English are: *If I were rich, I would buy a house. If it were nice out, we could go to the park.* Colloquially, we tend to say "If I was . . . ."

Hint!

Knowing when to use a verb in the subjunctive is manageable and need not be scary. First, the forms must be memorized as for any tense. Once vocabulary and verb forms are in your head, you can use them! Next, the key is to look at the main clause expressions. These are used repeatedly and will always require the subjunctive when you see them.

Formation of the Present Subjunctive

The present subjunctive stem of regular verbs is identical to the present indicative: drop the **-are**, **-ere**, or **-ire** of the infinitive. The present subjunctive endings closely resemble those of the present indicative; however, notice that endings in **-a**, **-ano** (used for **-are** verbs in present indicative) are now associated with the **-ere** and **-ire** verbs. Third conjugation (**-ire**) verbs that take **-isc-** in the present indicative will again use the **-isc-** in the present subjunctive. Notice that for all verbs in this mood, the forms **io**, **tu**, and **lui/lei** are identical. Subjunctive forms are rarely used alone; normally, they are in a secondary clause, indicated in the models below by the word **che**.

	-are	-ere	-ire	-ire (isc)
Infinitive:	**parlare**	**vedere**	**dormire**	**capire**
Stem:	**parl-**	**ved-**	**dorm-**	**cap-**
che io	**parli**	**veda**	**dorma**	**capisca**
che tu	**parli**	**veda**	**dorma**	**capisca**
che lui/lei	**parli**	**veda**	**dorma**	**capisca**
che noi	**parliamo**	**vediamo**	**dormiamo**	**capiamo**
che voi	**parliate**	**vediate**	**dormiate**	**capite**
che loro	**parlino**	**vedano**	**dormano**	**capiscano**

In the following examples, notice how the main clause will be in the indicative; its subjective meaning requires the secondary verb to be in the subjunctive. There is no special way to translate these verbs in English: in English the indicative and subjunctive sound the same.

La nonna vuole che tu <u>apra</u> la finestra.
Grandmother wants you to open the window.
È importante che voi <u>ascoltiate</u> il professore.
It's important that you listen to the professor.
Ho paura che mio marito <u>torni</u> tardi.
I'm afraid that my husband will return late.

You Need to Know ✔

You have learned that the subject pronouns are not usually used in Italian because each verb ending shows the doer. In the subjunctive the same ending is used for more than one person. In the sentence **Laura desidera che <u>telefoni</u>**, the verb form **telefoni** has various possible subjects: **io, tu, lui, lei**, or even **Lei** formal.
Laura wants me to call.
(Literally, *Laura wants that I call.*)
Laura wants you (informal) *to call.*
Laura wants him to call.
Laura wants her to call.
Laura wants you (formal) *to call.*

When the subject of the secondary verb is not clear by context, the subject pronoun should be added for clarification.

Irregular Present Subjunctive Verbs

Many verbs in the present subjunctive have irregular stems for the **io, tu, lui/lei**, and **loro** forms; however, you will notice that these stems come directly from the **io** stem of the (irregular) present indicative. The stems for **noi** and **voi** forms of these verbs are regular, like the infinitive.

Infinitive:	**bere**	**dire**	**fare**	**potere**
Present Indicative (**io**):	**bevo**	**dico**	**faccio**	**posso**
Pres. Subjunctive Stem:	**bev-**	**dic-**	**facci-**	**poss-**
che io	**beva**	**dica**	**faccia**	**possa**
che tu	**beva**	**dica**	**faccia**	**possa**
che lui/lei	**beva**	**dica**	**faccia**	**possa**
che noi	**beviamo**	**diciamo**	**facciamo**	**possiamo**
che voi	**beviate**	**diciate**	**facciate**	**possiate**
che loro	**bevano**	**dicano**	**facciano**	**possano**

Other irregular verbs function in the same way. If you have learned the irregular present indicative, finding the irregular present subjunctive stem is easy. *Remember*: these forms are preceded by **che** or another conjunction. They are only very rarely used alone.

andare	che vada, vada, vada, andiamo, andiate, vadano
cogliere	che colga, colga, colga, cogliamo, cogliate, colgano
morire	che muoia, muoia, muoia, moriamo, moriate, muoiano
parere	che paia, paia, paia, pariamo, pariate, paiano
porre	che ponga, ponga, ponga, poniamo, poniate, pongano
rimanere	che rimanga, rimanga, rimanga, rimaniamo, rimaniate, rimangano
salire	che salga, salga, salga, saliamo, saliate, salgano
scegliere	che scelga, scelga, scelga, scegliamo, scegliate, scelgano
tradurre	che traduca, traduca, traduca, traduciamo, traduciate, traducano
uscire	che esca, esca, esca, usciamo, usciate, escano
valere	che valga, valga, valga, valiamo, valiate, valgano
venire	che venga, venga, venga, veniamo, veniate, vengano
volere	che voglia, voglia, voglia, voliamo, voliate, vogliano

Other verbs in the present subjunctive are more irregular. Their stems must be memorized.

avere	che abbia, abbia, abbia, abbiamo, abbiate, abbiano
essere	che sia, sia, sia, siamo, siate, siano
dare	che dia, dia, dia, diamo, diate, diano
dovere	debba, debba, debba, dobbiamo, dobbiate, debbano
sapere	sappia, sappia, sappia, sappiamo, sappiate, sappiano
stare	stia, stia, stia, stiamo, stiate, stiano

Bisogna che <u>dicano</u> la verità.
It's necessary that they tell the truth.
È important che (tu) <u>traduca</u> l'articolo.
It's important that you translate the article.
Speriamo che <u>escano</u> con noi.
We hope that they go out with us.
Credi che (lui) <u>venga</u>?
Do you believe he's coming?
Sono contenta che (lei) <u>stia</u> bene.
I'm happy that she's feeling well.

Verbs and Expressions That Require the Present Subjunctive
The key to knowing when to use a verb in the subjunctive consists of looking at the main clause. Many common verbs and expressions, no matter what their tense, will always require their dependent clause verb to be in the subjunctive. These expressions can be grouped by category to help learn them.

Verbs of will, desire, preference, suggestion, hope

desiderare *to desire, want*
insistere *to insist*
preferire (isc) *to prefer*
sperare *to hope*
suggerire (isc) *to suggest*
volere *to want*

Voglio che tu <u>venga</u> qui.
I want you to come here.
Desiderano che io <u>parli</u> più spesso.
They want me to speak more often.
Preferisci che io <u>arrivi</u> alle due?
Do you prefer that I arrive at two o'clock?
Suggerisce che voi <u>partiate</u> presto.
He (she) suggests that you leave early.

Verbs and expressions of doubt, uncertainty

> **credere** *to believe*
> **dubitare** *to doubt*
> **pensare** *to think*
> **non è certo che** *it's not sure that*
> **non è vero che** *it's not true that*

> **Dubiti che Marco <u>sposi</u> con Marisa.**
> *You doubt that Mark is marrying Marisa.*
> **Non è certo che la famiglia lo <u>sappia</u>.**
> *It's uncertain whether the family knows.*

However, with expressions of certainty in the main clause, the present indicative is used.

> **È vero che <u>partono</u> insieme domenica.**
> *It's true that they are leaving together on Sunday.*
> **Sono sicura che la luna non <u>è</u> fatta di formaggio.**
> *I am sure that the moon is not made of cheese.*

Verbs of emotion

> **avere paura** *to be afraid*
> **arrabbiarsi** *to get angry*
> **dispiacersi** *to be sorry*
> **essere contento (-a, -i, -e)** *to be happy*
> **essere sorpreso (-a, -i, -e)** *to be surprised*
> **essere triste (-i)** *to be sad*
> **temere** *to fear*

> **Mi dispiace che Lei <u>parta</u> così presto.**
> *I'm sorry that you* (formal) *are leaving so soon.*
> **Siamo sorpresi che tutti <u>siano</u> qui.**
> *We are surprised that everyone is here.*

Verbs expressing commands

> **comandare** *to command, to order*
> **esigere** *to demand*
> **ordinare** *to order, to command*
> **pretendere** *to demand*
> **richiedere** *to require, demand*

Pietro esige che tutto <u>sia</u> pronto.
Peter demands that everything be ready.
Il maestro richiede che tutti <u>facciano</u> i compiti.
The teacher requires that everyone do their homework.

Verbs granting or refusing permission

lasciare *to let, to allow*
consentire *to allow, to permit*
permettere *to permit, to allow*
proibire *to forbid, to prohibit*

La signora lascia che il gatto <u>esca</u>.
The lady lets (her) cat go out.
Proibisco che voi <u>torniate</u> tardi.
I forbid you to return late.

Impersonal Expressions
The subjunctive is required after many impersonal expressions that denote an element of subjectivity. "Impersonal" means there is no particular person indicated as the subject of these verbs. The present subjunctive forms of the verb must be used after these and other similar expressions:

È meglio che *It's better that*
È necesario che *It's necessary that*
Basta che *It's enough that*
Bisogna che *It's necessary that*
Conviene che *It's fitting that*
È bene (male) che *It's good (bad) that*
È essenziale che *It's essential that*
È giusto che *It's right that*
È (im)possibile che *It's (im)possible that*
È (im)probabile che *It's (im)probable that*
(Non) importa che *It's (not) important that*
È un peccato che *It's a shame that*
È raro che *It's rare that*
È difficile che *It's difficult that*

Non importa che <u>arrivino</u> tardi.
It doesn't matter that they are arriving late.

È probabile che <u>nevichi</u> fra poco.
It's probable that it will snow shortly.
Peccato che lei <u>sia</u> quasi sempre ammalata.
It's a shame that she is almost always sick.

You Need to Know ✔

The simplest way to remember whether a clause should use the subjunctive is: subjunctive implies subjectivity.

Other Words that Introduce the Subjunctive

All the models above used **che** to introduce the subjunctive. When this is the case, the subjunctive is in the second half of the sentence. Other words and conjunctions may be used to introduce a verb in any of the subjunctives. When these begin a clause, that clause may move to the beginning of the sentence.

Devo partire <u>nonostante che io abbia la febbre</u>.
<u>Nonostante che io abbia la febbre</u>, devo partire.
I must leave even though I have a fever.

The following subordinate conjunctions require the subjunctive. The **non** in some of these expressions does not indicate a negative meaning; it is simply part of the conjunction.

prima che *before*
dopo che *after*
finché (non) *until*
senza che *without*
non appena che *as soon as*
a meno che non *unless*

malgrado
nonostante che
benché } *although*
sebbene
quantunque

a patto che
purché } *provided that*

affinché
in modo che } *so that*

posto che
supposto che } *supposing that*

The subjunctive is also required after indefinite pronouns and adjectives since their quality of imprecision suggests a subjective, not factual state.

chiunque *whoever*
dovunque, ovunque *wherever*
qualunque *whatever*

Chiunque telefoni, non rispondo.
Whoever is telephoning, I'm not answering.
Risparmiano sempre soldi, dovunque vadano.
They always save money wherever they go.

Other Uses of the Subjunctive

Commands
The subjunctive alone may function as an indirect command.

Che venga qui immediatamente!
Let him (her) come here at once!
Che se ne vada in pace!
May he (she) go in peace!
Che sia così!
So be it!

Indefinite Antecedents
When the antecedent (the word to which the clause refers) is definite and a knowable commodity, the verb in the secondary clause will be indicative.

Conosco un dottore che <u>parla</u> italiano.
I know a doctor who speaks Italian.
Hanno assunto una segretaria che <u>sa</u> il russo.
They have hired a secretary who knows Russian.

When the antecedent is imprecise, unknown or possibly nonexistent, the subjunctive must be used in the secondary clause.

Ho bisogno di un dottore che <u>parli</u> italiano.
I need a doctor who speaks Italian.
Cerchiamo una segretaria che <u>sappia</u> il russo.
We are looking for a secretary who knows Russian.

With Relative Superlatives
With opinions that incorporate the relative superlative, the subjunctive is used in the relative clause because the superlative expression is considered a subjective exaggeration. This construction is very common in Italian.

È il giocatore più bravo <u>che conosca</u>.
He's the best player that I know.
Sono i vini più buoni <u>che esistano</u>.
They are the best wines that exist.
È il regalo più bello <u>che abbia mai ricevuto</u>.
It's the most beautiful gift that I've ever received.

With Negative Expressions
The subjunctive must also be used in a clause that modifies a negative word or expression. As with superlatives, such statements are considered an unrealistic exaggeration, this time to the negative extreme. Observe:

Non c'è nessuno <u>che mi capisca</u>.
There is no one who understands me.
Non c'è niente <u>che valga la pena</u>.
Nothing is worth the trouble.

Replacing the Subjunctive with an Infinitive Construction
When the subject of the dependent clause is the same as that of the main clause, the inifinitive is used. Only the verb in the main clause is conjugated, and it will be used in the indicative. Compare:

Different subjects: **Roberta spera che tu venga.**
Roberta hopes that you'll come.
I genitori vogliono che io riceva buoni voti.
My parents want me to get good grades.

Same subject: **Roberta spera di venire.**
Roberta hopes to come.
Voglio ricevere buoni voti.
I want to get good grades.

The infinitive construction may also be used after verbs denoting command, permission, refusal, and suggestion. When this happens, the subjunctive clause may be replaced by an indirect object preceded by **a** and may be followed by an infinitive introduced by **di**.

> **Non permetto che mio figlio fumi.** =
> **Non permetto a mio figlio di fumare.**
> *I don't allow my son to smoke.*

When the indirect object is replaced by its pronoun, the **a** is no longer necessary.

> **Vi suggerisco che arriviate presto.** =
> **Vi suggerisco di arrivare presto.**
> *I suggest that you (all) arrive early.*

Formation of the Past Subjunctive

We have seen that main clause verbs and expressions that indicate demands, hopes, wishes, beliefs, etc., require the secondary verb to be in the subjunctive form. In all the models above, the demand, hope, or opinion was expressed in the present time frame: *My parents want . . ., I don't allow . . . .* The secondary action that the main clause referred to was also happening in the present or yet to come: *My parents want me to get good grades* (now, always, in the future).

However, wants, beliefs, opinions, etc., may be expressed at any time about an action that also happens, will happen, or has happened at any time. Four forms of the subjunctive exist to describe actions happening at different points in time relative to when someone expresses an opinion about them. Study these examples:

> *Mary thinks that John will arrive tomorrow.*
> *Mary thinks that John is arriving later today.*
> *Mary thinks that John arrived yesterday.*
> *Mary thought that John was arriving the next day.*
> *Mary thought that John had arrived the previous day.*

When an opinion or belief is expressed in the present about an already completed action, the main clause verb will be in the present indicative and the secondary verb will be in the present perfect subjunctive.

> **Maria pensa che Giovanni <u>sia arrivato</u> ieri**.
> *Mary thinks* (present) *that John arrived* (past) *yesterday.*

The present perfect subjunctive is rarely used alone, but normally comes in the dependent clause. Its formation is similar to the present perfect indicative (**passato prossimo**). One uses the present subjunctive forms of **avere** or **essere** plus the past participle.

	*Verbs that take **avere***	*Verbs that take **essere***
che io	**abbia parlato**	**sia andato (-a)**
che tu	**abbia parlato**	**sia andato (-a)**
che lui	**abbia parlato**	**sia andato**
che lei	**abbia parlato**	**sia andata**
che noi	**abbiamo parlato**	**siamo andati (-e)**
che voi	**abbiate parlato**	**siate andati (-e)**
che loro	**abbiano parlato**	**siano andati (-e)**

> **Ti dispiace che <u>abbia parlato</u> così**.
> *You're sorry that he (she) spoke like that.*
> **Non crediamo che <u>siano andati</u> in Italia**.
> *We don't believe that they went to Italy.*

Formation of the Imperfect Subjunctive

The imperfect subjunctive (**imperfetto del congiuntivo**) describes an incompleted action in a past context. It must be used when the want, belief, opinion, etc., of the main clause is also expressed in the past.

Mary thought that John was arriving the next day.

In this model, *Mary thought* is clearly a past action. At the time this action (Mary's thought) happened, the other action (John's arrival) had not yet been completed. The main clause verb of emotion requires an indicative tense; in this case, the present perfect because the action took place in the past. Verbs of emotion require a subjunctive in the clause that follows. Since the second action is not yet completed, the form of the subjunctive used must be the imperfect.

Remember

Imperfect tenses describe incompleted, habitual, or continuing actions in the past.

Like the regular imperfect tense, the imperfect subjunctive has only one part to the verb: the stem and ending shows everything (doer, action, and time frame). The regular stem is formed by dropping only the **-re** from the infinitive and adding the endings: **-ssi, -ssi, -sse, -ssimo, -ste, -ssero**. This set of endings is used for all verbs. The infix **-isc-** is never used with this mood.

Infinitive:	**parlare**	**vedere**	**venire**
Stem:	**parla-**	**vede-**	**veni-**
che io	**parlassi**	**vedessi**	**venissi**
che tu	**parlassi**	**vedessi**	**venissi**
che lui/lei	**parlasse**	**vedesse**	**venisse**
che noi	**parlassimo**	**vedessimo**	**venissimo**
che voi	**parlaste**	**vedeste**	**veniste**
che loro	**parlassero**	**vedessero**	**venissero**

There are only a few verbs that have irregular stems in the imperfect subjunctive. Recall that the extra letters in these stems actually come from the old form of the infinitive: **bere** was once **bevere**, etc. Memorize these stems and then use the regular endings as shown above.

Infinitive	*Stem*	*Imperfect Subjunctive Forms*
bere	bev-	che io bevessi, che tu bevessi, che bevesse, etc.
dire	dic-	che io dicessi, che tu dicessi, che dicesse, etc.
fare	fac-	che io facessi, che tu facessi, che facesse, etc.
condurre	conduc-	che io conducessi, etc.
tradurre	traduc-	che io traducessi, etc.
trarre	tra-	che io traessi, etc.

A few verbs have highly irregular stems in the imperfect subjunctive and must be memorized.

Infinitive:	essere	dare	stare
Stem:	fo-	de-	ste-
che io	fossi	dessi	stessi
che tu	fossi	dessi	stessi
che lui/lei	fosse	desse	stesse
che noi	fossimo	dessimo	stessimo
che voi	foste	deste	steste
che loro	fossero	dessero	stessero

Here are models showing the use of the imperfect subjunctive after main clauses that are also in the past. Notice the range of choices for the main clause verbs includes any past tense (present perfect, imperfect, preterit) or the conditional. Recall also that the secondary action (expressed by the subjunctive) may be ongoing or hoped for, but is never completed or realized.

> **Ho voluto che i bambini <u>dormissero</u>.**
> *I wanted the children to sleep.*
> **Non volevano che tu lo <u>facessi</u> così presto.**
> *They didn't want you to do it so soon.*
> **Loredana suggerí che Luigi <u>partisse</u>.**
> *Loredana suggested that Louis leave.*
> **Vorrebbe che io <u>raccontassi</u> una storia.**
> *He (she) would like me to tell a story.*

With Expressions Contrary to Fact or Unlikely
The imperfect subjunctive is used following expressions that indicate an action contrary to fact or unlikely to happen. The imperfect subjunctive

is often preceded by these adverbs: **magari, pure, se solo,** etc. It may even be used alone to express such unlikely possibilities.

> **Magari vincessi un milione di dollari!**
> *Would that I could win a million dollars!*
> **Vincessi pure!**
> *If I would indeed win!*
> **Se solo vincessi!**
> *If only I would win!*
> **Se avessi la tua fortuna!**
> *If only I had your luck!*
> **Avessi la tua fortuna!**
> *I wish I had your luck!*

You Need to Know ✔

Many of the rules and special uses discussed in the *Present Subjunctive* section apply when using other forms of the subjunctive as well. This includes all the verbs, expressions, and conjunctions that require the subjunctive; uses of the subjunctive in relative superlatives or with expressions of negativity, etc. The choice of subjunctive is based on the tense of the main clause; other applications remain the same.

Formation of the Pluperfect Subjunctive

Like the pluperfect indicative, the pluperfect subjunctive (**trapassato del congiuntivo**) describes an action that was completed in the past before another action was done (*had done something*): *Mary thought that John had arrived on time.* Here, John's action (arriving) was to have been completed before Mary thought about it.

Like all perfect tenses, the pluperfect subjunctive is compound, consisting of two parts: the imperfect subjunctive forms of **avere** or **essere** plus the past participle.

	Verbs that take *avere*	Verbs that take *essere*
	parlare	**andare**
che io	**avessi parlato**	**fossi andato (-a)**
che tu	**avessi parlato**	**fossi andato (-a)**
che lui	**avesse parlato**	**fosse andato**
che lei	**avesse parlato**	**fosse andata**
che noi	**avessimo parlato**	**fossimo andati (-e)**
che voi	**aveste parlato**	**foste andati (-e)**
che loro	**avessero parlato**	**fossero andati (-e)**

As with the imperfect subjunctive, the pluperfect subjunctive is used when the main clause verb is in the past or the conditional.

Ero sorpresa che <u>avessero detto</u> tali cose.
I was surprised that they had said such things.
Credeva che <u>fossimo ritornati</u> ieri.
He (she) thought that we had arrived yesterday.
Avrebbe preferito che tu gli <u>avessi telefonato</u> prima.
He (she) would have preferred that you had telephoned first.

"If" Clauses
For describing contrary-to-fact, uncertain, or hypothetic situations, Italian makes a distinction between greater and lesser degrees of probability. The English translation of such sentences does not accurately reflect this difference, and the English tenses used do not always correspond to Italian usage. Study the following models:

Uncertain outcome, high degree of probability

Vado in Italia se ho i soldi. (Present → Present)
I'm going to Italy if I have the money. (Present → Present)

Andrò in Italia se avrò i soldi. (Future → Future)
I will go to Italy if I have the money. (Future → Present)

Uncertain outcome, low degree of probability

Andrei in Italia se avessi i soldi. (Conditional → Imperf. Subjunctive)
I would go to Italy if I had the money. (Conditional → Preterit)

Sarei andata in Italia se avessi avuto i soldi.
(Past Cond. → Pluperfect Subjunctive)
I would have gone to Italy if I had had the money.
(Past Cond. → Pluperfect)

In the first two models, **se** (*if*) almost has the value of **quando** (*when*): **Vado in Italia quando ho i soldi**. (*I'm going to Italy <u>when</u> I have the money.*) In the second two models, the choice of conditional mood plus subjunctive show that this is a highly unlikely possibility. When hypothetical situations are discussed, Italian always uses the conditional in the main clause followed by either imperfect subjunctive or pluperfect subjunctive in the secondary clause.

Reflexive and Reciprocal Verbs

Reflexive Verbs

A reflexive verb expresses an action performed and received by the same subject: *I dressed myself.* Not all verbs can be used reflexively, but many verbs can have both meanings: *I washed the car* (nonreflexive), but *I washed myself* (reflexive). Reflexive verbs are used more frequently in Italian and other languages than in English.

In Italian, a reflexive verb is easily spotted: the pronoun **si** is attached to its infinitive after the final **-e** has been dropped: **lavarsi** (*to wash oneself*), **mettersi** (*to put on [clothing]*), **vestirsi** (*to dress oneself*). A set of reflexive pronouns corresponds to the subject doing the action and must always be used when this meaning is intended. (See Chapter 8: Pronouns, for more rules about how pronouns are used.)

When conjugating reflexive verbs, the pronoun **si** must first be detached, next moved in front of the verb, and finally converted to match the subject before adding the proper tense ending to the verb stem. The informal forms of reflexive pronouns may be attached to infinitives or imperatives. Here are examples of three regular reflexive verbs in the present indicative tense:

Infinitive:	lavarsi	mettersi	vestirsi
Verb Stem:	lav-	mett-	vest-
io	mi lavo	mi metto	mi vesto
tu	ti lavi	ti metti	ti vesti
lui/lei	si lava	si mette	si veste
noi	ci laviamo	ci mettiamo	ci vestiamo
voi	vi lavate	vi mettete	vi vestite
loro	si lavano	si mettono	si vestono

Mi lavo le mani prima di mangiare.
I wash my hands before eating.
Perché **ti metti** una cravatta?
Why are you putting on a tie?
Quelle donne **si vestono** elegantemente.
Those women dress themselves elegantly.
Spero di **laurearmi** l'anno prossimo.
I hope to graduate from university next year.
Lavati prima di uscire!
Wash yourself before going out!

You Need to Know ✔

Reflexive verbs are formed the same way as any other verb; they simply add a pronoun to indicate the notion of doing the action for oneself. This notion, although not complicated, is often unexpressed or implied in English, and may or may not be translatable. The reflexive pronouns and their translations follow:

mi = *myself*
ti = *yourself* (familiar)

cont. p. 110

cont.

si = *himself, herself, itself, yourself* (formal)
ci = *ourselves*
vi = *yourselves* (familiar)
si = *themselves, yourselves* (formal)
When conjugating reflexive verbs, the subject pronouns (**io, tu, lui, lei**, etc.) may be omitted, but the reflexive pronouns (**mi, ti, si**, etc.) must <u>always</u> be used to convey the proper meaning.

Here is a partial list of common reflexive verbs in Italian:

addormentarsi *to fall asleep*
arrabbiarsi *to get angry*
chiamarsi *to be named, "called"*
coprirsi *to cover oneself*
diplomarsi *to get a high school diploma*
divertirsi *to have fun, to enjoy oneself*
farsi il bagno *to take a bath*
farsi la doccia *to take a shower*
farsi male *to hurt oneself*
fidanzarsi (con) *to get engaged (to)*
innamorarsi (di) *to fall in love (with)*
lamentarsi (di) *to complain (about)*
laurearsi *to graduate from university*
pettinarsi *to comb one's hair*
radersi *to shave*
ricordarsi (di) *to remember (to)*
scusarsi *to excuse oneself*
sedersi *to sit down*
sentirsi *to feel*
sposarsi (con) *to get married (to)*
svegliarsi *to wake up*

Reflexive verbs may be conjugated in any tense or mood. In compound tenses, always use **essere** with reflexives since there is no direct object. In compound tenses, the reflexive pronoun, verb ending, and past

participle all must agree with the subject. Observe how the reflexive verb
divertirsi is conjugated in the **passato prossimo**:

io	**Mi sono divertito (-a)**.	*I had fun*. (= *I had a good time*.)
tu	**Ti sei divertito (-a)**.	*You had fun*.
lui	**Si è divertito**.	*He had fun*.
lei	**Si è divertita**.	*She* (*you,* formal) *had fun*.
noi	**Ci siamo divertiti (-e)**.	*We had fun*.
voi	**Vi siete divertiti (-e)**.	*You guys had fun*.
loro	**Si sono divertiti (-e)**.	*They* (*you,* formal) *had fun*.

Here are examples of the reflexive verb **alzarsi** in various tenses:

Present Indicative
> **Mi alzo alle sei**. *I get up at six (o'clock)*.

Present Perfect
> **Mi sono alzato (-a) alle sei**. *I got up at six*.

Imperfect Indicative
> **Mi alzavo alle sei**. *I used to get up at six*.

Preterit
> **Mi alzai alle sei**. *I got up at six*.

Pluperfect
> **Mi ero alzato (-a) alle sei**. *I had gotten up at six*.

Future
> **Mi alzerò alle sei**. *I will get up at six*.

Conditional Present
> **Mi alzerei alle sei**. *I would get up at six*.

Present Subjunctive
> **Credi che mi alzi alle sei?** *Do you think I get up at six?*

Past Subjunctive
> **Credi che mi sia alzato (-a) alle sei?**
> *Do you think I got up at six?*

Imperfect Subjunctive
> **Credevi che mi alzassi alle sei.**
> *You thought that I was getting up at six.*
> (or) . . . *that I used to get up at six.*

Pluperfect Subjunctive
Hai saputo che mi fossi alzato (-a) alle sei.
You found out that I had gotten up at six.

Reciprocal Verbs

Reciprocal verbs function the same way as reflexives, but involve only the plural forms: **noi, voi, loro**. A reflexive verb shows that the subject did an action for him- or herself; a reciprocal verb shows that two or more people exchanged the action. Some common reciprocal verbs follow.

abbracciarsi *to embrace each other (one another)*
aiutarsi *to help each other*
amarsi *to love one another*
baciarsi *to kiss each other*
conoscersi *to get to know one another*
incontrarsi *to meet each other (for an appointment)*
innamorarsi *to fall in love with one another*
rispettarsi *to respect each other*
rivedersi *to see each other again*
salutarsi *to greet each other*
scriversi *to write to each other*
telefonarsi *to phone each other*
vedersi *to see one another*
volersi bene *to care about one another*

Giuseppe e Maria si vedono spesso.
Joseph and Mary see each other often.
Paolo e Francesca si incontravano ogni venerdì sera.
Paul and Frances used to meet every Friday evening.
I buoni amici si aiutano.
Good friends help one another.
Io e i miei genitori ci vogliamo bene.
My parents and I care a lot about each other.

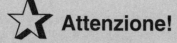

Attenzione!

Elision of reflexive pronouns mostly occurs in the case of **si** before another bright vowel (**e, i**): **si incontrano** → **s'incontrano, si innamorano** → **s'innamorano**. It may happen with other pronouns or vowels, especially in rapid speech. Elision (dropping a final vowel and adding an apostrophe) never occurs before a consonant. When in doubt, write it out!

The Imperative (Familiar and Formal)

Imperatives are used to make commands or give orders to other people. These have both familiar (**noi, voi, tu**) and formal (**Lei, Loro**) forms. The familiar forms are very similar or even identical to the present indicative tense whereas formal forms use the present subjunctive forms. Commands may be affirmative (telling someone to do something) or negative (telling someone <u>not</u> to do something). Subject pronouns are never used with commands; however, reflexive pronouns are attached to the end of the informal commands.

The **noi** and **voi** commands are exactly like present indicative:

	noi: *affirmative*	*negative*
cantare	**Cantiamo!** *Let's sing!*	**Non cantiamo!** *Let's not sing!*
mangiare	**Mangiamo!** *Let's eat!*	**Non mangiamo!** *Let's not eat!*
scriversi	**Scriviamoci!**	**Non scriviamoci!**
	Let's write each other.	*Let's not write each other!*
salire	**Saliamo!** *Let's go up!*	**Non saliamo!** *Let's not go up!*

	voi: *affirmative*	*negative*
	Cantate! *Sing!*	**Non cantate!** *Don't sing!*
	Mangiate! *Eat!*	**Non mangiate!** *Don't eat!*

Scrivetevi!	**Non scrivete!**
Write each other!	*Don't write each other!*
Salite! *Go up!*	**Non salite!** *Don't go up!*

The familiar **tu** commands (for giving orders to one person in an informal context) resemble the present indicative with two exceptions: the ending for all **-are** verbs is **-a** (looks like the normal ending for **lui/lei**) and the negative command is always formed with **non** + infinitive.

	tu: *affirmative*	*negative*
-are	**Canta!** *Sing!*	**Non cantare!** *Don't sing!*
-are	**Mangia!** *Eat!*	**Non mangiare!** *Don't eat!*
-ere	**Scrivi!** *Write!*	**Non scrivere!** *Don't write!*
-ire	**Sali!** *Go up!*	**Non salire!** *Don't go up!*
-isc-	**Finisci!** *Finish!*	**Non finire!** *Don't finish!*

These common verbs have certain irregular affirmative forms for **tu** and **voi**. The forms for **voi** not shown are regular. **Noi** is always regular present indicative: **-iamo**.

Infinitive:	**tu**	**voi**
andare	**Va'!**	—
dare	**Da'!**	—
dire	**Di'!**	—
fare	**Fa'!**	—
stare	**Sta'!**	—
avere	**Abbi!**	**Abbiate!**
essere	**Sii!**	**Siate!**
sapere	**Sappi!**	**Sappiate!**

Formal commands (**Lei**, **Loro**) are addressed to one or more persons in a formal setting. Most forms are identical with the present subjunctive forms of all verbs, including the irregular ones. Observe the following affirmative formal commands:

Infinitive:	**Lei**	**Loro**
parlare	**Parli!**	**Parlino!**
cantare	**Canti!**	**Cantino!**
vendere	**Venda!**	**Vendano!**
scrivere	**Scriva!**	**Scrivano!**
partire	**Parta!**	**Partano!**
finire	**Finisca!**	**Finiscano!**
andare	**Vada!**	**Vadano!**
avere	**Abbia!**	**Abbiano!**
bere	**Beva!**	**Bevano!**
essere	**Sia!**	**Siano!**
fare	**Faccia!**	**Facciano!**
dare	**Dia!**	**Diano!**
sapere	**Sappia!**	**Sappiano!**
stare	**Stia!**	**Stiano!**

The same forms are used for negative formal commands; simply add
non before the verb.

Lei	**Loro**
Non parli!	**Non parlino!**
Non canti!	**Non cantino!**
Non venda!	**Non vendano!**
Non scriva!	**Non scrivano!**

For giving formal commands with reflexive or reciprocal verbs, the
pronoun comes before the conjugated verb.

> **Si sieda, signore!** *Sit down, sir!*
> **Si alzi presto! Si alzino presto!** *Get up early!*
> **Si scrivano, care signore!** *Write to each other, dear ladies!*
> **Non si vesta casualmente!** ⎫
> **Non si vestano casualmente!** ⎭ *Don't dress casually!*

The Gerund vs. the Infinitive

The Present Gerund

In English the present gerund is the form of the verb that ends in *-ing*. In Italian, the gerund (*il gerundio*) of **-are** verbs ends in **-ando**.

Infinitive	Stem	Gerund
parlare	parl-	parlando
cantare	cant-	cantando
mangiare	mangi-	mangiando
cominciare	cominci-	cominciando
studiare	studi-	studiando
pagare	pag-	pagando

The present gerund of regular **-ere** and **-ire** verbs uses the present tense stem plus **-endo**. There is no **-isc-** in gerund formation.

credere	cred-	credendo
leggere	legg-	leggendo
aprire	apr-	aprendo
capire	cap-	capendo
finire	fin-	finendo

Irregular gerund stems resemble the present indicative **io** form:

bere	bev-	bevendo
dire	dic-	dicendo
fare	fac-	facendo
tradurre	traduc-	traducendo
trarre	tra-	traendo

The present gerund used alone in a clause indicates *while doing something*, *by means of doing something*.

> **Camminando**, ho incontrato Carlo.
> *While walking, I met Carl.*
> **Studiando**, Paolo impara molto.
> *By studying, Paul is learning a lot.*

Essendo amici, abbiamo parlato francamente.
Being friends, we spoke frankly.

The Past Gerund

The past gerund is formed with the present gerund of **avere** (**avendo**) or **essere** (**essendo**) plus the past participle (**-ato, -uto, -ito**) of the acting verb. Remember that **avere** is used when the verb takes a direct object; then the participle does not agree. If a direct object pronoun is used, the participle will agree with the object. When the verb is intransitive, **essere** must be used and the participle agrees with the subject. Pronouns, if any, will attach to the past gerund.

Avendo pranzato, **Pietro andò al cinema**.
Having dined, Peter went to the movies.
Avendola veduta, **l'abbiamo salutata**.
Having seen her, we greeted her.
Essendo arrivata presto, Anna Maria ha dovuto aspettare.
Having arrived early, Ann Marie had to wait.

Caution!

In forming the past gerund, Italian uses either **avere** (*to have*) or **essere** (*to be*) depending on whether the verb is transitive or intransitive; however, English always uses "having." Be careful of this when translating from English to Italian.

Progressive Tenses

Since you know how the present and imperfect indicative tenses work, and how to form the gerund, you can easily form the present and imperfect progressives. In Italian, these are used to emphasize the verb in a sentence and stress the action. They best translate: *to be in the process of doing something* or *to be doing something this very moment.*

The present progressive is formed by using the present indicative of **stare** plus the present gerund.

	cantare	scrivere	pulire
io	sto cantando	sto scrivendo	sto pulendo
tu	stai cantando	stai scrivendo	stai pulendo
lui/lei	sta cantando	sta scrivendo	sta pulendo
noi	stiamo cantando	stiamo scrivendo	stiamo pulendo
voi	state cantando	state scrivendo	state pulendo
loro	stanno cantando	stanno scrivendo	stanno pulendo

Sto studiando i verbi italiani.
I am (in the process of) studying the Italian verbs.
Stiamo ascoltando un nuovo CD.
We're listening to a new CD just now.

The imperfect progressive stresses that a particular action was going on at a particular moment in the past. Since this describes an ongoing action, the imperfect forms of **stare** are used plus the gerund.

	parlare	mettere	finire
io	stavo parlando	stavo mettendo	stavo finendo
tu	stavi parlando	stavi mettendo	stavi finendo
lui/lei	stava parlando	stava mettendo	stava finendo
noi	stavamo parlando	stavamo mettendo	stavamo finendo
voi	stavate parlando	stavate mettendo	stavate finendo
loro	stavano parlando	stavano mettendo	stavano finendo

Stavo lavando i piatti quando hai telefonato.
I was (in the process of) washing dishes when you called.
Stavamo salendo in macchina.
We were getting in the car (just then).

Uses of the Infinitive

Where English most often uses the present gerund, Italian more often uses the infinitve. *Compare*: **Gli ho parlato prima di <u>partire</u>**. BUT: *I spoke to him before <u>going</u> out.*

In infinitive constructions in Italian, the infinitive is frequently preceded by a preposition such as **per, prima di, senza**, etc. **Siamo pronti per uscire**. *(We are ready to go out.)* **Sono partiti senza dire niente**. *(They left without saying anything.)*

The construction **stare per** + infinitive means *to be about to do something*: **Stiamo per partire**. *(We are about to leave.)* **Sta per piovere**. *(It's about to rain.)*

The past infinitive is used after **senza** and **dopo**. It is common to drop the final **-e** of the auxiliary (**avere** or **essere**) in the past infinitive for pronunciation reasons: **aver cenato, esser venuti**.

> **Sono venuti senza aver telefonato.**
> *They came without having telephoned.*
> **Sono ritornati dall'Italia senza esser stati a Venezia.**
> *They returned from Italy without having been in Venice.*
> **È andato a teatro dopo aver comprato i biglietti.**
> *He went to the theater after having bought the tickets.*

Unlike English, the Italian infinitive may also function as a noun: **Viaggiare stanca**. *(Traveling is tiring.)* **Dormire poco fa male alla salute**. *(Sleeping little is bad for your health.)*

Italian also uses infinitives to give instructions in the affirmative in impersonal situations.

> **Rivolgersi alla porta indietro!** *Go to the back door!*
> **Spingere!** *Push!*
> **Tirare!** *Pull!*
> **Tenere la destra!** *Keep right!*
> **Tenere la sinistra!** *Keep left!*
> **Tenersi lontano!** *Keep off! (Keep away!)*

For impersonal commands or instructions in the negative, the infinitive is often preceded by the past participle **vietato** (*forbidden*).

> **Vietato entrare!** *No entrance!*
> **Vietato fumare!** *No smoking!*
> **Vietato girare a destra (a sinistra)!** *No right (left) turn!*
> **Vietato sostare!** ⎫
> **Sosta vietato!** ⎬ *No parking! or No stopping!*

The Infinitive after Verbs of Permission and Perception
Letting, seeing, watching, listening, or hearing someone do something is expressed by the conjugated forms of **lasciare, vedere, guardare, ascoltare,** or **sentire** plus the infinitive.

> **Ho lasciato giocare i bambini.** *I let the children play.*
> **Hai visto cadere la bambina.** *You saw the girl fall.*
> **Ascoltavo suonare Fabrizio.** *I was listening to Fabrizio play.*
> **Ho sentito cantare Patrizia.** *I heard Patricia sing.*

Fare in Causative Constructions (*far fare*)
Fare plus another verb in the infinitive indicates that the subject is *having* or *has had* an action performed by someone else.

> **Fa studiare i ragazzi.** *She makes the boys study.*
> **Hai fatto riparare la macchina.** *You had the car repaired.*
> **Facevamo costruire la casa**. *We were having the house built.*

If the object is a noun, it always follows the infinitive. When an object pronoun is used, however, it precedes the verb **fare**.

> **Faccio studiare i ragazzi.** → **Li faccio studiare.**
> **Hai fatto riparare la macchina.** → **L'hai fatta riparare.**

When a causative sentence has two objects, the person being made to do something becomes the indirect object and is usually introduced by the preposition **a**. However, for clarity the preposition **da** may be used, Observe:

One object:	**Il maestro fa leggere lo studente.**
	The teacher is having (making) the student read.
Two objects:	**Il maestro fa leggere il brano allo studente.**
	The teacher is having the passage read to (or by) the student.
For clarity:	**Il maestro fa leggere il brano <u>da</u>llo studente.**
	The teacher is having the passage read by the student.

The Passive Voice (*Voce Passiva*)

Although the passive voice is considered a weak construction in English, it is used frequently in Italian. It is formed with the conjugated forms of **essere** (any tense) plus the past participle of the acting verb. Since **essere** is used, the participle must agree with its subject. The direct object of the active voice sentence becomes the subject in the passive voice. The agent or person who performs the action is introduced by the preposition **da** (when necessary, contracted with the definite article). Compare the following sentences.

Active Voice: **Il postino distribuisce le lettere.**
                  The mail carrier is delivering the letters.
Passive Voice: **Le lettere sono distribuite dal postino**.
                  The letters are being delivered by the mail carrier.

Active Voice: **Gina ha mandato i pacchi**.
                  Gina sent the packages.
Passive Voice: **I pacchi sono stati mandati da Gina**.
                  The packages were (have been) sent by Gina.

Active Voice: **La signora comprerà il biglietto.**
                  The lady will buy the ticket.
Passive Voice: **Il biglietto sarà comprato dalla signora.**
                  The ticket will be purchased by the lady.

The Passive Voice with *si*

A common way to form the passive in Italian is by using the reflexive pronoun **si** with the third-person singular or plural form of the verb (**lui/lei, loro**). This construction is common when the agent of the action is unstated or unimportant, or when the action is habitual.

    Qui si parla italiano.
    Italian is spoken here. (Literally, *here Italian speaks itself.*)
    In quel negozio si vendono camicie e cravatte.
    In that store shirts and ties are sold.

Chapter 6
NEGATIVE WORDS AND CONSTRUCTIONS

IN THIS CHAPTER:

✔ *Negative Sentence Formation*
✔ *Common Negative Expressions*
✔ *Negation of Compound Tenses*

Negative Sentence Formation

The most common way to make a sentence negative in Italian is to insert the word **non** before the conjugated verb.

> **Voglio dormire**. *I want to sleep.*
> **Non voglio dormire**. *I do not want to sleep.*
>
> **Abbiamo finito**. *We have finished.*
> **Non abbiamo finito**. *We haven't finished.*

If there are any object pronouns before the verb, **non** precedes the pronoun.

> **Marcella la conosco**. *Marcella knows her.*
> **Marcella non la conosco**. *Marcella doesn't know her.*
>
> **Ce l'abbiamo fatta**. *We did it.*
> **Non ce l'abbiamo fatta**. *We didn't do it.*

Common Negative Expressions

Adding **non** to a sentence simply negates its meaning. To convey a more precise emotional charge to the negation, a second word must be used after the verb. In effect, this is a double negative which would be considered "bad grammar" if translated into English verbatim, but is perfectly correct in Italian.

> <u>Non</u> faccio <u>niente</u> stasera.
> (Literally, *I'm not doing nothing this evening.*)
>
> <u>Non</u> viaggi <u>mai</u> in aereo.
> (Literally, *You don't never travel by plane.*)

The following common negative expressions work the same way. As is often the case in Italian, some have more than one version with no difference in meaning and may be used interchangeably.

non . . . ancora	*not yet*
non . . . che	*only*
non . . . mai	*never*
non . . . né . . . né	*neither . . . nor*
non . . . nessuno	*no one, nobody*
non . . . più	*no longer*

non . . . niente (standard Italian) ⎱ *nothing*
non . . . nulla (Florentine) ⎰

non . . . affatto
non . . . mica ⎱ *not at all*
non . . . punto ⎰

non . . . neanche
non . . . nemmeno ⎱ *not even*
non . . . neppure ⎰

To be even more emphatic, the second term of some of these expressions may begin a sentence; when this happens, **non** is dropped.

> <u>Nessuno</u> ha mandato un regalo. *No one sent a gift.*
> <u>Niente</u> è nel frigo. *Nothing is in the fridge.*

<u>Mai</u> viaggiamo in aereo. *Never do we travel by plane.*
<u>Né</u> Giovanni <u>né</u> Maria ha telefonato.
Neither John nor Mary telephoned.

As in English, more than one negative element may appear in a single sentence. The **non** is used only once.

Carlo non dice <u>mai</u> <u>niente</u> a <u>nessuno</u>.
Carl never says anything to anyone.

You Need to Know ✔

Nessuno (*no one*) used alone is a pronoun and does not agree. **Nessun(o)** may also be used as an adjective to mean "not a single . . . ." In this case, it always precedes the noun, is always in the singular, and will make agreements like the indefinite article: **ness<u>un</u>, ness<u>uno</u>, ness<u>una</u>, ness<u>un</u>'**.

Non ho mangiato <u>nessuna</u> pasta.
I didn't eat a single pastry.
Non ho comprato <u>nessun</u> ricordo.
I didn't buy a single souvenir.
Non ho visto <u>nessun'amica</u>.
I didn't see a single female friend.

Negation of Compound Tenses

With any compound past tense (present perfect, past conditional, pluperfect, etc.), the second word of most of these expressions follows the past participle.

Non hanno trovato nessuno.
They didn't find anyone.
Non abbiamo visto nessuna ragazza.
We didn't see a single girl.
Non ci hanno detto niente.
They didn't tell us anything. (= They said nothing to us.)
Non ha trovato né il passaporto né i biglietti.
He (she) found neither the passport nor the tickets.

With the negative expressions that use **affatto**, **ancora**, **mai**, and **più**, the second term is often inserted between the auxiliary and the past participle:

> **Luigi non ha lavorato affatto.** ⎫
> **Luigi non ha affatto lavorato.** ⎬ *Louis didn't work at all.*
>
> **Non sono stata mai in Russia.** ⎫
> **Non sono mai stata in Russia.** ⎬ *I've never been in Russia.*

The combinations **non . . . mica** and **non . . . punto** usually come between the auxiliary and the past participle:

> **Non ha <u>mica</u> parlato.** *He hasn't spoken at all.*
> **Non è <u>punto</u> partito.** *He hasn't left at all.*

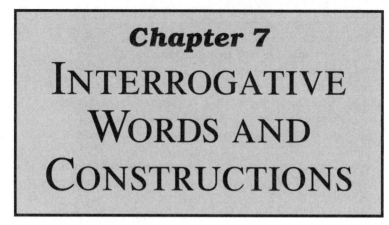

Chapter 7
INTERROGATIVE WORDS AND CONSTRUCTIONS

Question Formation in Italian

In Italian there are three ways of forming a question: (1) by intonation, i.e., simply raising the voice at the end of a normal statement; (2) by inversion, i.e., moving the subject to the end of the sentence and raising the voice; or (3) by adding a tag phrase to a question that most likely has an affirmative answer. Unlike English, questions in Italian never begin with *do* or *does, don't or doesn't.* Compare the following statements made into questions:

	Statement	*Question*
1.	**Sergio compra libri.**	**Sergio compra libri?**
	Sergio is buying books.	*Is Sergio buying books?*
	Avete una grande casa.	**Avete una grande casa?**
	You (two) have a big house.	*Do you have a big house?*
2.	**Sergio compra libri.**	**Compra libri Sergio?**
	Sergio is buying books.	*Is Sergio buying books?*
	Voi avete una grande casa.	**Avete una grande casa voi?**
	You (two) have a big house.	*Do you two have a big house?*
3.	**Sergio compra libri.**	**Sergio compra libri, non è vero?**

Sergio is buying books, isn't he?

Avete una grande casa.   **Avete una grande casa, no?**

You (two) have a big house, right?

Remember

Italian questions that will probably be answered "yes" can be formed by simply adding a tag phrase to the end and raising the voice. Tag phrases are: **no**?, **non è vero**?, **è vero**?, **vero**? or the phonetic contraction **nevvero**? These translate *"doesn't he (she, it)?," "right?"* or *"isn't that so?"*

Interrogative Expressions

The question formation methods shown above elicit a simple yes or no response. For more specific information in the answer, other interrogative words and expressions begin the question. The most common interrogatives adverbial expressions follow.

A che ora? *At what time?*	**Quando?** *When?*
Come? *How? How's that?*	**Quanto?** *How much?*
Come mai? *How come? Why ever?*	**Perché?** *Why?*
Dove? *Where?*	**Di dove?** *From where?*

With all of these except **Come mai?** the inverted question form is used.

With Inversion
A che ora partono i tuoi amici?
At what time (hour) are your friends leaving?
Come sta Guido? *How is Guido?* (health)
Com'è Firenze? *What is Florence like?* (description)
Dove sono i bambini? *Where are the children?*
Quando usciamo? *When (hour, day or date) will we go out?*
Quanto costa quest'anello? *How much does this ring cost?*

BUT

No Inversion
Come mai Mario non è qui? *How come Mario isn't here?*

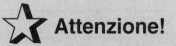

Attenzione!

Perché means both *why* and *because*. A question that begins with **Perché** may also be answered with the same word in the response. Vocal inflection is used to distinguish the two: **Perché piangi**? (*Why are you crying*?) **Perché sono triste.** (*Because I'm sad.*)

Interrogative Pronouns

Che, Chi

The interrogative pronouns **che** (*what*) and **chi** (*who, whom*) can be used as subjects, direct objects, or objects of a preposition. These pronouns always come at the beginning of a question when used as interrogatives. Observe the following examples:

Che succede? *What's happening?*
Chi ha telefonato? *Who telephoned?*
Chi cerchi? *Whom are you looking for?*
Di chi parlano? *Whom are they talking about?*
Di che parlano? *What are they talking about?*
Di chi è questa giacca? *Whose is this jacket?*

There are three interchangeable ways to begin a question with "what":

<u>Che</u> **fai stasera?**
<u>Che cosa</u> **fai stasera?** } *What are you doing this evening?*
<u>Cosa</u> **fai stasera?**

Quale, Quali

Quale (*which*) or **quali** (*which ones*) is another common interrogative pronoun. For purposes of agreement, this shows only number, not gender. Note that the singular form drops the final **-e** before **è** or **era**, and the apostrophe is no longer used: **qual**. The plural form **quali** never elides.

Quale dei libri preferisci?
Which (one) of the books do you prefer?
Qual è il tuo libro preferito?
Which is your favorite book?
Quali leggi? *Which ones do you read?*

Interrogative Adjectives

Quale, -i

Quale (*which*) can also be used as an adjective to describe nouns. It agrees only in number (sing. or plur.) with the noun.

Con quale ragazzo esci? *Which guy do you go out with?*
Quale canzone ti piace? *Which song do you like?*
Quali gruppi ti piacciono? *Which groups do you like?*
Quali ragazze inviti? *Which girls are you inviting?*

Unlike English, there is a slight difference in meaning between Italian **che** and **quale**. **Che** refers to a precise person or thing and elicits only one correct answer; **quale** allows for a range of choices.

Che giorno è oggi? *What day is it today?*
Quale vino preferisci? *Which (of many) wine do you prefer?*
Quali CD comprano? *Which (of many) CDs are they buying?*

Quanto (-a, -i, -e)

The interrogative adjective **quanto (-a, -i, -e)** means "how much" in the singular and "how many" in the plural. It always precedes the noun it modifies and must agree in gender and number.

Quanto pane hanno consumato?
How much bread have they consumed?
Quanta farina rimane? *How much flour is left?*
Quanti turisti visitano Venezia ogni anno?
How many tourists visit Venice each year?
Quante mele desidera, signora?
How many apples do you want, ma'am?

IN THIS CHAPTER:

- ✔ *Direct Object Pronouns*
- ✔ *Indirect Object Pronouns*
- ✔ *Disjunctive Pronouns*
- ✔ *The Particle* **Ne**
- ✔ *Double Object Pronouns*
- ✔ *The Adverb of Place* **Ci**
- ✔ *Relative Pronouns*
- ✔ *Adjectives with Pronomial Forms*

Pronouns take the place of a noun and are used to eliminate redundant repetition of the same words in a sentence, paragraph, or conversation. Notice how clumsy communication would be without pronouns: *Did you see the film? Yes, I saw the film. Did you like the film? No, I didn't really like the film.*

In Italian as in English, different types of pronouns reflect their grammatical function. For subject pronouns and reflexive pronouns, see Chapter 5. The present chapter introduces various other types: direct object pronouns, indirect object pro-

nouns, disjunctive pronouns, and even the adverbial expression **ci** that functions as a pronoun. Sometimes Italian uses a pronoun where English would not, or a different category of pronoun than English does.

Remember that pronouns always replace something in order to simplify a subsequent statement. In Italian, all pronouns show gender and number so attention must be paid to make them agree with the word or words they replace. There are also basic rules for position, many of which will apply to more than one type of pronoun.

✳ Direct Object Pronouns

A direct object receives the action described by the verb and done by the subject. It answers the questions *Whom?* or *What?* In the sentence *Laura is reading the newspaper*, "the newspaper" is the direct object. ("What is Laura reading?" "The newspaper.") The direct object pronouns in Italian are listed below:

Singular	*Plural*
mi (*m.* or *f.*) *me*	**ci** (*m.* or *f.*) *us*
ti *you* (*m.* or *f.*, informal)	**vi** *you* (*m.* or *f.*, informal)
lo, l' (*m.*) *him, it*	**li** (*m.*) *them*
la, l' (*f.*) *her, it*	**le** (*f.*) *them*
La *you* (formal)	**Li, Le** *you* (formal)

To use a pronoun, first determine the direct object. Is it masculine or feminine, singular or plural? Then find the corresponding pronoun. In Italian, unlike English, the pronoun typically <u>precedes</u> the conjugated verb:

> **Laura legge <u>il giornale</u>. Laura <u>lo</u> legge.**
> *Laura is reading the newspaper. Laura is reading it.*
> **Giorgio usa <u>la scheda telefonica</u>. Giorgio <u>la</u> usa.**
> *George is using the phone card. George is using it.*
> **<u>Mi</u> chiami stasera? —Sì, <u>ti</u> chiamo.**
> *Will you call me this evening? —Yes, I'll call you.*
> **<u>Ci</u> invitate? —Certo che <u>vi</u> invitiamo!**
> *Are you inviting us? —Of course, we'll invite you!*

Before a verb that starts with a vowel or silent **h**, **lo** and **la** can elide: **Giorgio <u>l'</u>usa. L'** can be either *m.* or *f.* **Mi, ti, ci,** and **vi** may elide before bright vowels (**e, i**), especially in rapid conversation. **Li** and **le** never elide and must always be said or written out.

For formal address, the direct object pronouns are the third-person forms, capitalized in writing to indicate formality:

> **Signora, <u>La</u> ho conosciuta al convegno dell'anno scorso.**
> *Ma'am, I met you at last year's conference.*
> **Signori Pirri, <u>Li</u> aspetto davanti.** (No elision!)
> *Mr. and Mrs. Pirri, I'll wait for you out front.*

Often Italian uses the masculine singular pronoun **lo** (*it*) where English would not when referring to abstract concepts.

> **Credi che Giovanni venga? —Sì, <u>lo</u> credo.**
> *Do you think John will come? —Yes, I believe so.*
> **Sai che diamo una festa? —Sì, <u>lo</u> so.**
> *Do you know that we're throwing a party? —Yes, I know (it).*

Indirect Object Pronouns

The indirect object receives the action of a verb indirectly. It answers the questions *To whom?* or *For whom? To which?* or *For which?* In the sentence *I bought the flowers for my mother,* "for my mother" is the indirect object of the verb. ("For whom did you buy the flowers?" "For my mother.") The indirect object pronouns in Italian are shown below. The first four "persons" (**mi, ti, ci, vi**) are identical to the direct object pronouns. **Gli** means both *to him* (*m. sing.*) and *to them* (*m. or f. plur.*).

Singular	*Plural*
mi *to me*	**ci** *to us*
ti *to you* (informal)	**vi** *to you* (informal)
gli *to him*	**gli** *to them* (*m.* or *f.*)
le *to her*	also, **loro** *to them* (informal)
Le *to you* (formal)	**Loro** *to you* (formal)

> **<u>Mi</u> dai il libro?** *Will you give the book to me?*
> **Scrivo un messaggio <u>a Carlo</u>. <u>Gli</u> scrivo un messagio.**
> *I'm writing a message to Carl. I'm writing a message to him.*

Signora, riporto il modulo <u>a Lei</u>? <u>Le</u> riporto il modulo?
Ma'am, do I bring the form back to you?

Loro is really a subject pronoun that can also mean *to them* (*m.* or *f. pl.*, informal) or *to you* (*pl.*, formal). To show formality, it is often capitalized in writing. When used as an indirect object pronoun, **loro** always follows the verb.

Mandiamo il pacco <u>ai parenti</u>.
We're sending the package to the relatives.
<u>Gli</u> mandiamo il pacco. BUT: **Mandiamo <u>loro</u> il pacco.**
We're sending the package to them.

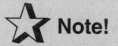 **Note!**

In English it can at times be difficult to differentiate the direct from the indirect objects. We may say "I'm writing Carl a letter" or "I'm writing a letter to Carl." The direct object is often a thing and the indirect object is often a person, but this is not a hard and fast rule. Italian always makes a clearer distinction between direct and indirect objects. The prepositions **a** (*to*) and **per** (*for*) indicate indirect objects.

Italian Verbs That Take Indirect Objects
Many common verbs in Italian require an indirect object where there is none in English. These include: **chiedere** (*to ask for*), **dire** (*to say, tell*), **domandare** (*to ask for*), **insegnare** (*to teach*), **rispondere** (*to reply*), **spiegare** (*to explain*), and **telefonare** (*to telephone*). A special effort must be made to remember these verbs.

Takes Direct Object	*Takes Indirect Object*
Ask the police officer!	**Chiedi <u>al</u> poliziotto!**
I'm answering the phone.	**Rispondo <u>al</u> telefono.**
She's phoning her mom.	**Telefona <u>alla</u> mamma.**

Disjunctive Pronouns

Normally, Italian pronouns precede the verb; however, for emphasis they may come after the verb. Special stressed forms (similar to subject pronouns) are used. These forms must also be used after prepositions, such as in comparisons. When stress pronouns are used, the emphasis shifts to that word. Asterisks indicate irregular forms.

Subject Pronouns	*Disjunctive Pronouns*
io	**me***
tu	**te***
lui	**lui**
lei	**lei**
Lei (formal)	**Lei**
noi	**noi**
voi	**voi**
loro	**loro**
Loro (formal)	**Loro**

Amo <u>te</u> e solo <u>te</u>. *I love you and only you.*
Stefano mi chiama sempre. Chiama <u>me</u> e non <u>lei</u>.
Stephen always calls me. He calls me and not her.
Sono meno pigro di te! *I am less lazy than you!*

Position of Object Pronouns

In Compound Tenses
Typically, Italian pronouns precede the conjugated verb. This includes reflexive and reciprocal pronouns. In compound tenses, the pronouns precede the auxiliary (**avere** or **essere**). When **avere** is used in compound tenses (i.e., the verb has a direct object), the past participle agrees in gender and number with the noun the pronoun has replaced.

Ci siamo incontrati allo zoo. *We met each other at the zoo.*
Ho visto le ragazze. Le ho viste. *I saw the girls. I saw them.*
Ha riportato i documenti a me. Li ha riportati a me.
He brought the documents back to me. He brought them back to me.

Indirect object pronouns also precede the auxiliary in compound tenses, but the past participle never agrees with them. *Remember*: **loro** as an indirect pronoun always follows the verb.

> **Ho dato la mela alla cavalla. Le ho dato la mela.**
> *I gave the apple to the mare. I gave the apple to her.*
> **L'agente ha dato i biglietti ai signori.**
> **Ha dato loro i biglietti.**
> *The agent gave the tickets to the gentlemen.*
> *The agent gave the tickets to them.*

With Infinitives
When infinitive constructions are used, most pronouns may be attached to the infinitive or precede the verb that accompanies the infinitive. When the pronoun is attached, the final **-e** of the infinitive is dropped.

Voglio darle la mela. OR **Le voglio dare la mela.**
I want to give the apple to her.
Li hai intenzione di comprare. OR **Hai intenzione di comprarli.**
You are planning to buy them.

With the Gerund
Any pronoun except **loro** may attach to a gerund (**-ando, -endo**). In progressive tenses, the pronoun may either precede the auxiliary **stare** or be attached to the gerund. *Remember*: gerunds never make agreements.

Mangiandolo, mi sentivo male.
While eating it, I felt sick.
Vedendola, il signore ha detto "Buon giorno!"
Upon seeing her, the gentleman said, "Good day!"
Sto leggendola. OR **La sto leggendo.**
I am in the process of reading it now.

Remember

Often Italian has more than one way of saying something, so many options can be confusing for the language learner! When confronted with equivalent expressions, you should be able to recognize all of them when you hear or read them. In speaking or writing, it is your choice. To simplify the situation, choose a favorite and use it all the time.

With Informal Commands
When a pronoun is used with informal commands (**tu**, **noi**, **voi**), it attaches to the end of the command. When this happens, the word becomes longer. Be careful to maintain the accent on the proper syllable of the verb (as it is said without the attached pronoun).

Cantala! Cantatela! Cantiamola!
Sing it! Sing it! Let's sing it!
Scrivilo! Scrivetelo! Scriviamolo!
Write it! Write it! Let's write it!
Finiscili! Finiteli! Finiamoli!
Finish them! Finish them! Let's finish them!
Alzati! Alzatevi! Alziamoci!
Get up! Get up! Let's get up!

In negative informal commands, the pronouns still attach to the verb. For negative **tu** commands, the pronoun may precede or attach to the infinitive after dropping the final **-e**.

noi   **Non alziamoci presto!** *Let's not get up early!*
voi   **Non mangiatelo!** *Don't eat it!*
tu   **Non mangiarlo!** OR **Non lo mangiare!** *Don't eat it!*

With monosyllabic **tu** commands (**da'**, **di'**, **fa'**, **sta'**, **va'**), all types of pronouns attach to the verb and double their first consonant (except for **gli**): **Dacci il CD!** (*Give the CD to us!*) **Dimmi!** (*Tell me!*) **Fallo!** (*Do it!*) **Stacci vicino!** (*Stay close to us!*) *Exception:* **Dagli i soldi!** (*Give the money to him!*)

With Formal Commands
Pronouns always precede the formal commands both in the affirmative and in the negative. This is true for any type of pronoun. **Mi dica!** (*Tell me!*) **Non lo faccia!** (*Don't do it!*) **Non gli mandi la lettera!** (*Don't send the letter to him!*) **Non le diano gli assegni!** (*Don't give her the checks!*) **Si accomodi**, **signora!** (*Make yourself comfortable, ma'am!*)

The Particle **Ne**

The particle **ne** works like a pronoun to replace the partitive, quantities, and prepositional phrases introduced by **di**. It means *some, any, about, of it, of them, from it*. It is invariable (shows no agreement) and can be used to replace nouns of any gender or number. It is used in the following instances:

To replace the partitive

Ho <u>del tempo libero</u>.	**Ne ho.**
I have some free time.	*I have some.*
Ha <u>delle verdure fresche</u>.	**Ne ha.**
She has some fresh vegetables.	*She has some.*

With quantities

Ha molti amici.	**Ne ha molti.**
He has many friends.	*He has many of them.*
Hai alcuni libri.	**Ne hai alcuni.**
You have some books.	*You have some of them.*
Ho quattro gatti.	**Ne ho quattro.**
I have four cats.	*I have four of them.*

When expressing quantities, **ne** only replaces the noun. Indefinite adjectives (**molti, alcuni, pochi**) or numbers must be stated.

To replace clauses beginning with **di**

Parliamo sempre di futbol.	**Ne parliamo sempre**.
We always talk about football.	*We always talk about it.*
Discutevamo di politica.	**Ne discutevamo**.
We were discussing politics.	*We were discussing it.*

To replace **di** *plus an infinitive*

Hanno paura di volare.	**Ne hanno paura**.
They are afraid of flying.	*They're afraid of it.*
Ho voglia di domire.	**Ne ho voglia**.
I feel like sleeping.	*I feel like it.*

Double Object Pronouns

Many sentences have both a direct and an indirect object: *I bought the flowers for my mother*. Here, "the flowers" is direct and "for my mother" is indirect. It is possible to replace both with pronouns. Italian has special double object pronoun combinations to use in such cases. These are related to the normal pronouns, with certain vowel changes to facilitate pronunciation. In these combinations, the particle **ne** comes under the heading of "direct." Here is a chart of all the possibilities. The combinations must always be used in this order:

Direct → Indirect ↓	**lo**	**la**	**l'**	**li**	**le**	**ne**
mi → **me**	**me lo**	**me la**	**me l'**	**me li**	**me le**	**me ne**
ti → **te**	**te lo**	**te la**	**te l'**	**te li**	**te le**	**te ne**
gli → **glie-** ⎫ le → **glie-** ⎬ Le → **glie-** ⎭	**glielo**	**gliela**	**gliel'**	**glieli**	**gliele**	**gliene**
ci → **ce**	**ce lo**	**ce la**	**ce l'**	**ce li**	**ce le**	**ce ne**
vi → **ve**	**ve lo**	**ve la**	**ve l'**	**ve li**	**ve le**	**ve ne**
gli (*plur.*)	*Same as for singular. See above.*					

Mio padre me li dà. *My father gives them to me.*
Te lo presto domani. *I'll loan it to you tomorrow.*
Ce ne portavano. *They were bringing us some of it.*
Ve l'ha insegnata. *He (she) taught it to you guys.*

You Need to Know ✔

In double object pronoun combinations, all third-person forms (*m.*, *f.*, *sing.*, and *pl.*) will use the form **glie-** + the direct object pronoun. **Glielo** expresses all these meanings: *it to him, it to her, it to you* (formal), or *it to them*. **Glie-** is the only double pronoun form that has the indirect object attached to it: **Glielo do.** *I'll give it to him* (*to her; to you formal; or to them*).

To express *to them,* it is also possible to use **loro**. However, **loro** must follow the verb and never combines with direct object pronouns. Compare: **Ho dato loro i biglietti. Glieli ho dati. = Li ho dati loro.** (*I gave the tickets to them. I gave them to them.*)

When reflexive or reciprocal pronouns are used in double object pronoun combinations, they always take the position of the indirect pronoun and precede the direct pronoun. **Si** becomes **se** before another pronoun and is not attached: **se lo, se la, se li, se le, se ne.** **Se** can mean *for* or *by himself, for herself, for yourself* (formal), or *for themselves.*

> **Mi lavo le mani.** → **Me le lavo.**
> *I wash my hands. I wash them.*
> **Ci mandiamo delle cartoline.** → **Ce ne mandiamo.**
> *We're sending each other some postcards.*
> *We're sending some to each other.*

Note that with reflexive verbs in compound tenses, the past participle agreement may change, depending on the nature of the pronoun that precedes the verb. The participle will agree with the subject only if the reflexive pronoun is used. When a direct object pronoun is inserted, the participle must agree with it. (*Remember*: the participle <u>never</u> agrees with indirect object pronouns.)

> **Mi sono lavata le mani.** → **Me <u>le</u> sono lavat<u>e</u>.**
> *I washed my hands.* → *I washed them.*
> **Ti sei fatto la barba.** → **Te <u>la</u> sei fatt<u>a</u>.**
> *You shaved your beard.* → *You shaved it.*

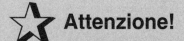 **Attenzione!**

The common expression **Ecco!** (from Latin, *Behold!*) is used to point out or indicate something actually present before the speaker. Frequently, it is used with pronouns. When this is the case, the pronouns always attach:

Eccomi! *Here I am!*
Eccolo! *Here (There) he (it) is!*
EccoLa! *Here (There) you (formal) are!*
Eccoci! *Here we are!*
Eccoli! ⎫ *Here (There) they are!*
Eccole! ⎭

Ecco can be used in various combinations with one or more object complements:

Eccoti il libro! *Here's the book for you!*
Eccotelo! *Here it is for you!*
Eccovene! *Here are some for you guys!*
Eccogliene! *Here are some for him (her)!*
Eccogliene, signora! *Here are some for you, ma'am!*
BUT
Ecco Loro le lettere! *Here are the letters for you!*

The Adverb of Place Ci

You may have noticed that in Italian a single word can mean more than one thing. **Ci** can be a direct object pronoun (*us*), indirect object pronoun (*to us*), reflexive pronoun (*for ourselves*), or reciprocal pronoun (*to each other*). **Ci** (or the less frequent **vi**) is used in the common verb **esserci** (*to be there*): **c'è** (*there is*), **ci sono** (*there are*). The meaning *there* makes **ci** useful for replacing adverbial clauses that begin with **a**, **da**, **in**, or **su** to indicate a place or location. The adverb **ci** works just like a pronoun, but it never changes or makes agreements.

> **Guido va a Bologna.** → **Guido ci va.**
> *Guido is going to Bologna. Guido is going there.*
> **Andate da Mirella? Ci andate?**
> *Are you all going to Mirella's place?*
> *Are you going there?*
> **Viviamo bene in America.** → **Ci viviamo bene.**
> *We live well in America. We live well there.*
> **Il micio è salito sul tetto. Ci è salito.**
> *The kitten climbed up on the roof. It climbed up there.*

By extension, **ci** is also used to replace abstract or conceptual clauses that begin with **a**, **da**, **in**. **Credi nell'oroscopo?** → **No, non ci credo.** *(Do you believe in the horoscope? No, I don't believe in it.)* **Comincio a lavorare alle otto.** → **Ci comincio alle otto.** *(I start to work at eight. I start [it] at eight.)*

Relative Pronouns

Pronouns in general replace redundant words and make communication more elegant. Relative pronouns are used to link two sentences that share a common element into a single sentence. In the following models, "the girl" is a common element: *I saw the girl. Caitlin is the girl.* By replacing "the girl" with a relative pronoun, a single, smooth sentence results: *Caitlin is the girl whom I saw.* Here, "the girl" (*whom*) is the direct object of the verb *saw*.

Che

In Italian, the relative pronoun **che** (*that, which, who, whom*) replaces either a person or a thing. It functions as either the subject or direct object of a clause. **Che** does not show gender or number; it never changes. Observe how it unites two sentences into one:

> **Vedo la ragazza. La ragazza è la sorella di Robertino.** →
> **La ragazza che vedo è la sorella di Robertino.**
> *The girl whom I see is Robbie's sister.*

Che can represent either the subject or direct object of a clause.

> **Il giovane che parla è molto intelligente.** (subject)
> *The young man who is talking is very intelligent.*
> **Ti piace la gonna che sto portando?** (direct obj.)
> *Do you like the skirt I'm wearing?*

Cui

A different relative pronoun must be used instead of **che** when replacing the indirect object or a prepositional phrase. **Cui** (*to whom, for whom, to which, for which*) is also invariable (never changes) and can refer to people or things. **Cui** is most often preceded by a preposition. Here are some possibilities with their meanings:

cui = a cui *to whom, to which*	**per cui** *for whom, for which*
con cui *with whom, with which*	**da cui** *from whom, from which*
di cui *of whom, of which*	**su cui** *on whom, on which*
in cui = dove *in whom, in which*	

> **La signora per cui ho fatto il favore è la mia vicina.**
> *The lady for whom I did the favor is my neighbor.*
> **Gli amici di cui parlavamo sono in Italia.**
> *The friends of whom we were speaking are in Italy.*

Quel(lo) che, ciò che

The relative pronouns **quello che, quel che,** or **ciò che** are used to replace a general or abstract idea rather than a specific antecedent. They are similar to English *what* or *that which*. They may be used interchangeably:
Non capisco quello che dici. (*I don't understand what you are saying.*)
Quel che ti consiglio è di fumare di meno. (*What I suggest to you is to smoke less.*) **Ciò che dici non è vero.** (*What you're saying is not true.*)

144 ITALIAN

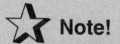 **Note!**

When **cui** is used alone, its meaning is the same as **a cui** (*to whom, to which*): **Ecco l'uomo (a) cui ho dato l'opuscolo**. *(There's the man to whom I gave the pamphlet.)*

To refer to places in which something happened, **in cui** or **dove** may be used interchangeably: **Il ristorante <u>in cui</u> abbiamo cenato era abbastanza lontano.** = **Il ristorante <u>dove</u> abbiamo cenato era abbastanza lontano.** (*The restaurant in which [= where] we dined was quite far off.*)

Cui preceded by the definite article means *whose*. The article will agree with the noun that follows **cui: Ecco la signora <u>il cui</u> fratello è psicologo.** (*Here's the lady whose brother is a psychologist.*)

Il (la) quale, i (le) quali

The pronoun **quale, -i** plus the definite article (**il, la, li, le**) at times replaces **che** or **cui** either to lend emphasis or to avoid ambiguity. However, unlike **che** or **cui**, **il quale** must agree in gender and number with the noun it replaces. It can refer to people or things and has various meanings: *the one(s) who, the one(s) which*. If a preposition is needed, it will contract with the definite article.

> **L'articolo <u>di cui</u> hai parlato era interessante.** =
> **L'articolo <u>del quale</u> hai parlato era interessante.**
> *The article about which you spoke was interesting.*
> **La scrittrice <u>che</u> darà la conferenza è molto famosa.** =
> **La scrittrice <u>la quale</u> darà la conferenza è molto famosa.**
> *The author who will give the lecture is very famous.*

Adjectives with Pronominal Forms

In Chapter 3, you learned about indefinite, possessive, and demonstrative adjectives. Many of these can be made into pronouns with no change of meaning simply by dropping the noun they modify. When used as pronouns, they still must agree in gender and number with the noun they have now replaced. Adjectives that end in -uno agree with their nouns, but are *m. sing.* when used alone as pronouns. Observe:

As Adjectives	*As Pronouns*
Non vedo <u>nessun</u> amico.	**Non vedo <u>nessuno</u>**.
I don't see a single friend.	*I don't see anyone.*
Hai comprato <u>alcuni</u> biscotti.	**Hai comprato <u>alcuni</u>**.
You bought some cookies.	*You bought some.*
Ti presto <u>la mia</u> penna.	**Ti presto <u>la mia</u>**.
I'll loan you my pen.	*I'll loan you mine.*
Mi piace <u>questo</u> cappotto.	**Mi piace <u>questo</u>**.
I like this coat.	*I like this one.*

You Need to Know ✔

When possessive pronouns (**il mio**, **la tua**, etc.) are used after the verb **essere**, the definite article is usually omitted except for **loro**:

Questa casa è mia. *This house is mine.*
Quello è suo. *That one is his (hers, its).*
Quella valigia è la loro. *That suitcase is theirs.*

Other Relative Pronouns
Chi can be used as a relative pronoun meaning *one who*, especially in proverbs. It always takes a singular, third-person verb and is considered masculine for purposes of agreement: **Chi studia, impara**. *(One who studies, learns.)* **Chi dorme, non piglia pesci**. *(He who sleeps catches no fish.)*

Alternate phrases that express this are: **colui che** (*he who*), **colei che** (*she who*), and **coloro che** (*those who*). **Colui** and **colei** take a singular verb; **coloro** requires a plural verb: <u>Colui che</u> **entra è mio fratello**. *(He who [the one who] is entering is my brother.)* <u>Colei che</u> **entra è mia sorella**. *(She who is entering is my sister.)* <u>Coloro che</u> **entrano sono i miei fratelli**. *(Those who are entering are my brothers.)*

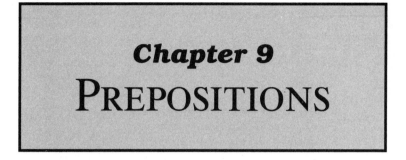

Chapter 9
PREPOSITIONS

IN THIS CHAPTER:

✔ *Special Uses of* **a**, **in**, **da**, *and* **di**
✔ *Verbs That Take* **a** *or* **di** *before an Infinitive*

Special Uses of **a**, **in**, **da**, and **di**

Prepositions are used in Italian to indicate a variety of concepts such as possession, distance, origin, intention, etc. The prepositions **a**, **in**, **da**, and **di**, however, can have rather specific uses in Italian. They acquire different meanings in different constructions. Prepositions do not always translate directly from one language to another; often, the precise meaning is influenced by the accompanying verb.

Special Uses of *a*
The preposition **a** usually means *to* or *at*. However, before the name of a town or city, it can mean *in*.

> **(andare) Vado a Milano**. *I'm going to Milan.*
> BUT
> **(essere) Sono a Milano per tre giorni**.
> *I'll be in Milan for three days.*
> **(studiare) Giovanni studia a Pisa**.
> *John is studying in Pisa.*

(vivere) **La loro nonna vive a Crotone**.
Their grandmother lives in Crotone.

In Italian the preposition **a** is also used with distance from a certain place.

Il museo è due chilometri da qui.
The museum is two kilometers from here.
I miei nonni abitano a cinque miglia.
My grandparents live five miles (away).

Since Italian rarely forms compound nouns, **a** is also used in adverbial clauses that describe fabric designs or materials.

una giacca a righe *a striped jacket*
una gonna a fiori *a flowered skirt*
un vestito a quadri *a checkered suit*
un sacco a pelo *a sleeping bag* (literally, "sack of hair")

A is also used to describe natural modes of transportation.

Ti piace andare a cavallo? *Do you like to ride horseback?*
Vado a scuola a piedi. *I go to school on foot.*

Special Uses of *in*
The Italian preposition **in** often corresponds to English *in*, especially after the verb **essere** with continents, countries, regions, and states.

La Libia è in Africa. *Libya is in Africa.*
Roma è in Italia. *Rome is in Italy.*
Tallahassee è in Florida. *Tallahassee is in Florida.*

If the country, region, or state is modified by an adjective, or is masculine, the definite article must be used and attaches to **in**. Remember that **in** becomes **ne-** when attached to the article.

Abitiamo negli Stati Uniti. *We live in the United States.*
Ti piacerebbe abitare nel Canadà?
Would you like to live in Canada?

Molte persone vanno nel Colorado per sciare.
Many people go to Colorado to ski.

In is used to speak of artificial, mechanical modes of transportation. Its meaning here changes to *by*.

in aereo *by plane*   **in macchina** *by car*
in bicicletta *by bicycle*   **in barca** *by (small) boat*
in treno *by train*

With many common locations such as rooms of a house, shops, etc., **in** is used without the definite article to express *in, into,* or *to*. With such locations, English expresses *the*; Italian drops it.

in città *in (into) the city*   **in ufficio** *in the office*
in montagna *in the mountains*   **in chiesa** *in (to) church*
in campagna *in (into) the country*   **in giardino** *in the garden*
in salotto *in the living room*   **in bagno** *in the bathroom*
in cucina *in the kitchen*   **in biblioteca** *in the library*

Vado <u>in</u> biblioteca. *I'm going <u>to</u> the library.*
BUT
Ho studiato <u>in</u> biblioteca. *I studied <u>in</u> the library.*

Preposition usage can be frustrating because meanings do not always correspond directly between languages. When a usage differs from grammatical structures you already know, special effort must be made to memorize it. After repeated encounters, such usages do become more automatic.

Special Uses of *Da*

The Italian preposition **da** most often has the English meaning *from*: **Stanno tornando da Catania**. (*They are returning from Catania.*)

Before a personal noun or pronoun, **da** means *at someone's house or place of business*: **Mia figlia è dal dottore**. (*My daughter is at the doctor's.*) **Andremo da Paola stasera?** (*Shall we go to Paula's this evening?*)

After a disjunctive pronoun (**me, te, sé, noi, voi**), **da** means *by myself, by yourself*, etc. **L'ho fatto da me**. (*I did it by myself*). **Franco ha finito la lezione da sé**. (*Frank finished the lesson by himself.*)

Da before an infinitive or noun describes the purpose, function, suitability, or use of the noun. Again, this is done because Italian cannot simply use two nouns together.

> **Ho bisogno della carta da scrivere.**
> *I need some writing paper* (lit., *paper for writing*).
> **Mangiamo sempre nella sala da pranzo.**
> *We always eat in the dining room* (lit., *room for dining*).

Da before an infinitive conveys the notion of an action that remains *to be done*. It may also denote a need or obligation that something *must be done*.

> **Avete due libri da leggere.**
> *You have two books to read (that must be read).*
> **Ci sono tre stanze da affittare.**
> *There are three rooms to rent.*

Da is also frequently used before an infinitive and after **molto, poco, niente, troppo, tanto, qualcosa** (**qualche cosa**). This construction also implies that something remains to be done.

> **Abbiamo tanto da fare.** *We have so much to do.*
> **Non c'è niente da mangiare.** *There's nothing to eat.*

Da before a noun describes the style of a person's behavior, manner, or comportment, equivalent to English *like a* (*as a*).

> **Mi tratta da principessa.** *He treats me like a princess.*
> **Mi hai sempre parlato d'amico.**
> *You've always spoken as a friend to me.*

Da may also follow a noun or adjective to describe physical characteristics or qualities of a person. English would use *with*.

> **Chi è il giovanotto dai capelli biondi?**
> *Who is the young man with the blonde hair?*
> **Chi è quella ragazza dagli occhi verdi?**
> *Who is that girl with the green eyes?*

You have learned that in the passive voice, **da** is used to show the agent of an action. Here, it has the meaning *by*.

> **La città fu distrutta da un terremoto.**
> *The city was destroyed by an earthquake.*
> **L'edificio è stato disegnato dall'architetto.**
> *The building was designed by the architect.*

In Italian **da** is used after a noun to indicate price or value.

> **un francobollo da 0,77 euro** *a postage stamp worth .77 euro*
> **un film da quattro soldi** *a "two-bit" (low-quality) movie*

Da in temporal expressions is equivalent to English *when* or *since*. Such constructions imply continuous, ongoing actions so the present indicative or imperfect indicative tenses are used.

> **Studio l'italiano da due mesi.**
> *I've been studying Italian for two months (since two months).*
> **Da bambino aveva molti giocattoli.**
> *As a child (since he was a child), he had many toys.*

Special Uses of *Di*

The Italian preposition **di** normally corresponds to English *of*. It is used before nouns, pronouns, proper names, or professional titles to express possession.

> **È la macchina di Giorgio.** *It's George's car.*
> **Dov'è l'ufficio del dottore?** *Where is the doctor's office?*

The Italian **di** for possession also indicates origin, in the sense that a person belongs to his or her native region: **Sei di Ravenna.** (Literally: *You are of Ravenna*; *You are Ravenna's*.)

Because Italian does not form compound nouns, **di** is used after nouns to indicate the materials or substances that they are *made of*: **un orologio d'oro** (*a golden watch*); **una giacca di lana** (*a woolen jacket*).

Di is used after the indefinite pronouns **qualcosa** and **niente** (**nulla**) and before the adjective that modifies them. Note that in this construction, the adjective always takes the *m. sing.* form: **qualcosa di bello** (*something lovely*), **qualcosa di buono** (*something good*), **niente di nuovo** (*nothing new*). The **di** is not translated.

Many expressions that refer to times or seasons use **di**.

> **di mattino** *in the morning*
> **del pomeriggio** *in the afternoon (p.m.)*
> **di sera** *in the evening*
> **di notte** *at night, by night*
> **di buon'ora** *early*
> **di giorno** *in the daytime, by day*
> **d'estate** *in the summer*
> **d'inverno** *in the winter*

In speaking of artistic creation or intellectual property, **di** has the meaning of *by*.

> **un quadro di Botticelli** *a painting by Botticelli*
> **una sinfonia di Mozart** *a symphony by Mozart*
> **un'opera di Verdi** *an opera by Verdi*
> **un romanzo di Moravia** *a novel by Moravia*

Verbs That Take **a** or **di** before an Infinitive

Many Italian verbs require the preposition **a** before an infinitive (unconjugated verb form). Others take **di**. Still others do not require any preposition, but are followed immediately by an infinitive. In reading or listening, the meaning of such constructions is usually clear, although sometimes meanings are idiomatic (not directly translatable) and must be memorized. Here are some common examples; the lists below are not exhaustive.

Verbs That Take *a* before an Infinitive

abituarsi a *to get used to*	**imparare a** *to learn*
aiutare a *to help*	**insegnare a** *to teach to*
cominciare a *to begin*	**insistere a** *to insist*
continuare a *to continue*	**mettersi a** *to begin to, to start*
divertirsi a *to have fun (by doing something)*	

> **Adesso comincio a capire i verbi.**
> *Now I am beginning to understand verbs.*
> **Finalmente siamo riusciti a risolvere il problema.**
> *Finally we managed to solve the problem.*

Verbs That Take *di* before an Infinitive

Many verbs take **di** before an infinitive. Here are some:

accettare di *to accept*	**lamentarsi di** *to complain*
ammettere di *to admit*	**ricordar(si) di** *to remember*
cercare di *to try, attempt*	**smettere di** *to stop doing . . .*
decidere di *to decide*	**suggerire di** *to suggest*
dimenticare di *to forget*	**vantarsi di** *to brag about*

> **Abbiamo sognato di essere in un film.**
> *We dreamed of being in a film.*
> **Offrono di pagare il conto.**
> *They are offering to pay the check.*

Verbs Followed Directly by an Infinitive

Modal verbs (**dovere, potere, volere**) and certain other verbs are always used before an infinitive with no intervening preposition.

amare *to love*	**occorrere** *to be necessary*
ascoltare *to listen to*	**osare** *to dare*
bastare *to suffice*	**parere, sembrare** *to seem*
bisognare *to be necessary*	**piacere** *to please*
gradire *to appreciate*	**preferire** *to prefer*

> **Basta lavorare otto ore al giorno.**
> *It's enough to work eight hours a day.*
> **Desideriamo vivere in pace.**
> *We want to live in peace.*

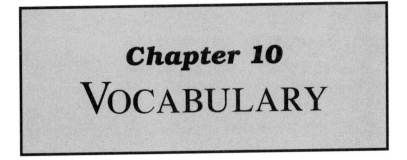

Chapter 10
VOCABULARY

All'aeroporto

Figure 10-1

Figure 10-2

All'albergo

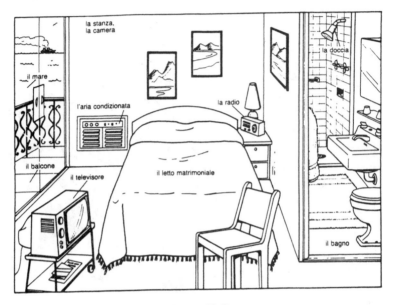

la stanza,
la camera

il mare

l'aria condizionata

la radio

la doccia

il balcone

il televisore

il letto matrimoniale

il bagno

Figure 10-3

il banco registrazione *registration desk*
la chiave *the key*
al completo *full, "no vacancy"*
la conferma *confirmation*
i documenti *identity documents*
il modulo di registrazione *registration form*
il passaporto *passport*
la colazione *breakfast*
il ragazzo d'albergo *bellboy*
il servizio *service*
le tasse *taxes*
vito e alloggio *room and board*

All'albergo

Figure 10-4

l'aria condizionata *air conditioning*
"Avanti!" ("Entri!") *"Come in!"*
l'asciugacapelli *hair dryer*
la carta igienica *toilet paper*
il cassettone *chest of drawers*
il comodino *night stand*
il letto singola *twin bed*
il letto matrimoniale *double bed*
il materasso *the matress*
la saponetta *bar of soap*
il sapone *soap*
il servizio guardaroba *laundry service*
il supplemento *surcharge*
la sveglia *the alarm clock*
il W.C. *water closet, bathroom*

A casa

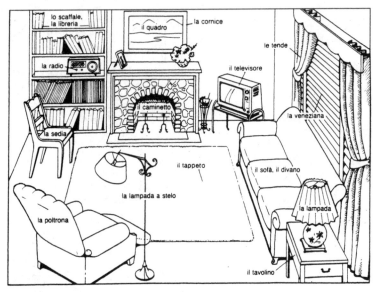

Figure 10-5

il bagno *bathroom*
il box, il garage *garage*
la camera da letto *bedroom*
il congelatore, il freezer *freezer*
la credenza *sideboard*
la cucina *kitchen*
il fornello *stove burner*
il forno *oven*
il frigo(rifero) *refrigerator*
il lavabo, il lavandino *sink*
la lavapiatti, la lavastoviglie *dishwasher*
la lavatrice *washing machine*
le matonelle *ceramic tiles*
la moquette *wall-to-wall carpeting*
il pavimento *the floor*
il rubinetto *faucet*
la sala da pranzo *dining room*
il salotto *living room*
la vasca da bagno *bathtub*
il videoregistratore *VCR*

A tavola

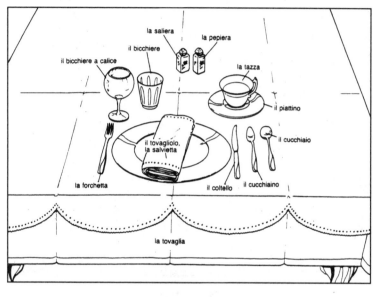

Figure 10-6

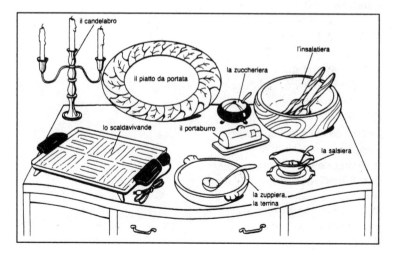

Figure 10-7

In banca

Figure 10-8

il Bancomat *ATM machine*
la banconota *banknote*
il biglietto da (5 euro) *paper money, bill, valued at (5 euros)*
il cambio *exchange rate*
la carta di credito *credit card*
la carta bancaria *bank card*
il centesimo *cent*
contanti *cash*
l'euro, gli euro *the euro(s)*
l'importo *amount, sum*
la moneta da . . . *coin valued at . . .*
il PIN (codice segreto) *PIN number*
il resto *change*
gli spiccioli *small change*
lo sportello *cashier's window*
l'ufficio di cambio *exchange bureau*
assegni da viaggio, traveller cheques *traveller's checks*

Alla spiaggia

Figure 10-9

l'abbronzatura *suntan*
il (la) bagnante *bather*
il capanno *cabana, cabin*
il cappello da spiaggia *beach hat*
il costume da bagno *swimsuit*
la crema solare *sunscreen*
il mare *the sea*
gli occhiali da sole *sunglasses*
l'onda *wave*
la pallavolo *volleyball*
il pallone *kick ball, soccer ball*
la sabbia *the sand*
gli sandali *sandals*
il sole *the sun*
la tintarella *suntan*
il telobagno *beach towel*
la villeggiatura *summer vacation*

Il corpo umano

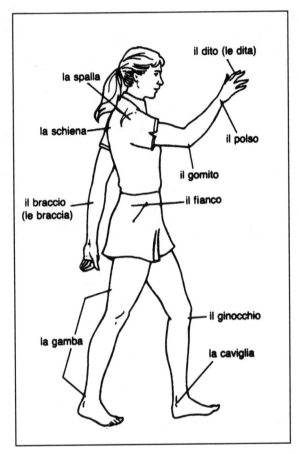

la spalla

il dito (le dita)

la schiena

il polso

il gomito

il braccio
(le braccia)

il fianco

il ginocchio

la gamba

la caviglia

Figure 10-10

la bocca *mouth*	**il labbro** (pl. **le labbra**) *lip(s)*
i capelli *hair*	**il naso** *nose*
il cuore *heart*	**l'occhio** *eye*
i denti *teeth*	**l'orecchio** *ear*
il dito del piede *toe*	**l'osso** (pl. **le ossa**) *bone(s)*
il dorso, la schiena *back*	**il petto** *chest*
la faccia, il viso *face*	**il piede** *foot*
il fegato *liver*	**il polmone** *lung*
il fianco *hip*	**il sangue** *blood*
la gola *throat*	**la testa** *head*

Il computer

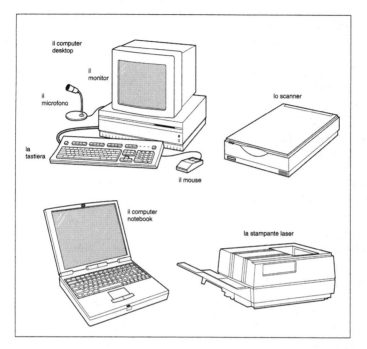

Figure 10-11

l'accessorio *peripheral*
l'allegato *attachment*
l'applicazione *application*
le cartelle *folders*
il database *database*
il disco rigido (fisso) *hard drive*
l'elaboratore di testi *word processor*
il file *file*
il foglio elettronico *spreadsheet*
la fonte *font*
la giustificazione *justification of text*
l'intestazione *heading*
l'ipertesto *hypertext*
la memoria *memory*
la posta elettronica, l'email *email*
lo schermo *viewing screen*
il sito web *web site*
lo slot di espansione *expansion slot*
le specifiche *specifications*

Il commercio

l'amministrazione *administration*
le attività *assets*
l'azione *share of stock*
gli azionisti *stockholders*
la bancarotta *bankruptcy*
i beni *goods*
il bilancio patrimoniale *balance sheet*
la Borsa *the stockmarket*
il commercio *business*
i compratori *buyers*
il dirigente *director*
la domanda e l'offerta *supply and demand*
l'entrata *income*
imprese commerciali *business enterprises*
il marketing *marketing*
le passività *liabilities*
il prezzo *price*
il prodotto *the product*
la produzione *production*
il profitto *profit*
la pubblicità *advertising*
il reddito *income*
i rendiconti *accounting statements*
la società per azioni (SpA) *corporation*
la società semplice *partnership*
il socio *business partner, associate*
le tasse *taxes*
vendere all'ingrosso *to sell wholesale*
vendere al minuto (al dettaglio) *to sell retail*
i venditori *sellers*

Index

165